Diagonal (or On-Point) Set

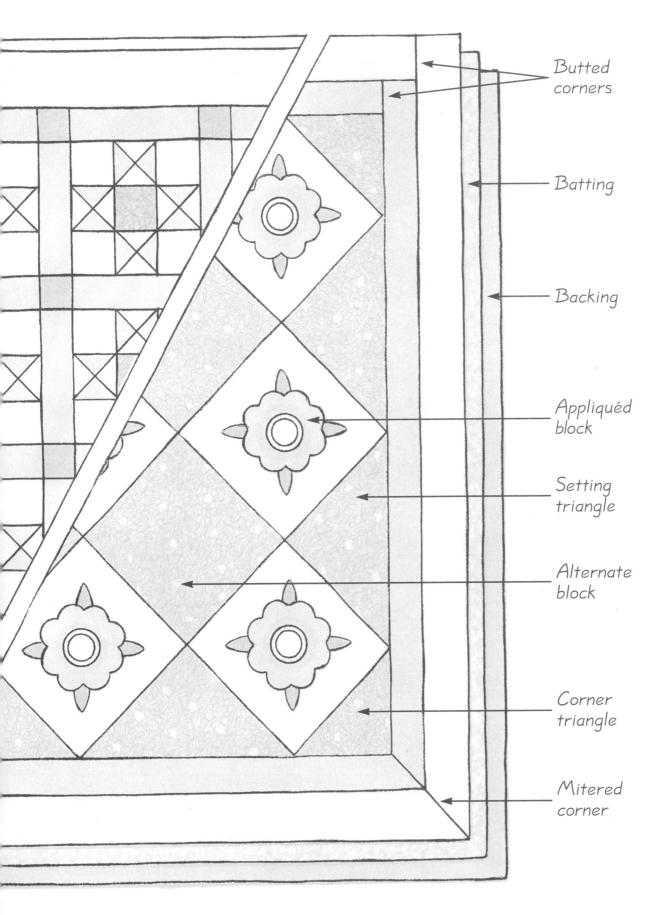

Butted corners

Batting

Backing

Appliquéd block

Setting triangle

Alternate block

Corner triangle

Mitered corner

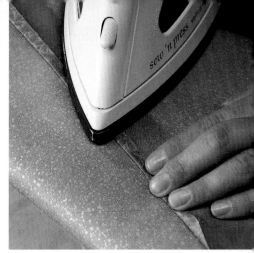

Rodale's Successful Quilting Library®

Fantastic Finishes

Sarah Sacks Dunn
Editor

Rodale Press, Inc.
Emmaus, Pennsylvania

OUR PURPOSE

*We inspire and enable people to improve
their lives and the world around them.*

The writers and editors who compiled this
book have tried to make all of the contents
as accurate and as correct as possible. Illustrations, photographs, and text have all been
carefully checked and cross-checked. However,
due to the variability of personal skill, tools,
materials, and so on, neither the writers nor
Rodale Press assumes any responsibility for any
injuries suffered or for damages or other losses
incurred that result from the material presented
herein. All instructions should be carefully
studied and clearly understood before
beginning any project.

Printed in the United States of America on
acid-free ∞ , recycled paper ♻

Editor: Sarah Sacks Dunn
Contributing Editor: Jane Townswick
Writers: Mimi Dietrich, Dixie Haywood,
   Becky Herdle, Susan McKelvey, Ann Seely,
   Joyce Stewart, Janet Wickell, and Darra
   Duffy Williamson
Book Designers: Sandy Freeman, Sue Gettlan,
   and Chris Rhoads
Layout Designer: Keith Biery
Illustrators: Mario Ferro and Sandy Freeman
Photographer: Mitch Mandel
Cover Photographer: John Hamel
Photo Direction and Stylist: Sandy Freeman
Photography Editor: James A. Gallucci
Models: Cathy Brooks and Erana
   Bumbardatore
Copy Editor: Candace B. Levy
Manufacturing Coordinator: Patrick Smith
Indexer: Nan Badgett
Editorial Assistance: Susan Nickol

Rodale Home and Garden Books
Managing Editor, Quilt Books:
   Suzanne Nelson
Director of Design and Production:
   Michael Ward
Associate Art Director: Carol Angstadt
Production Manager: Robert V. Anderson Jr.
Studio Manager: Leslie M. Keefe
Copy Director: Dolores Plikaitis
Manufacturing Manager: Mark Krahforst
Office Manager: Karen Earl-Braymer

We're always happy to hear from you.

For questions or comments concerning
the editorial content of this book, please
write to:

Rodale Press, Inc.
Book Readers' Service
33 East Minor Street
Emmaus, PA 18098

Look for other Rodale books
wherever books are sold. Or call us at
(800) 848-4735.

For more information about Rodale Press
and the books and magazines we publish,
visit our Web site at:
www.rodale.com

**Library of Congress Cataloging-in-Publication
Data published the first volume of this series as:**

Rodale's successful quilting library.
      p.   cm.
Includes index.
ISBN 0–87596–760–4 (hc: v. 1:alk paper)
1. Quilting. 2. Patchwork. I. Soltys, Karen
Costello. II. Rodale Press.
TT835.R622   1997
746.46'041—dc21   96–51316

Fantastic Finishes:
   ISBN 0–87596–821–X

**Distributed to the book trade
by St. Martin's Press**

   4   6   8   10   9   7   5   hardcover

Contents

Introduction

If every quilt tells a story, the last paragraph is its edge finish. It can shout jubilantly, sit shyly, or chuckle playfully. Or it can tell a whole story of its own. . . .

My own first attempt at quilting was a three-block Ohio Star table runner. I was taking an informal quilting class at work, and I forgot about patience being a virtue. As soon as I had my top pieced, I just couldn't wait for the next class, so I machine quilted it, then bound it, from memory, according to some sketchy directions in a book I had once read.

Well, I learned my lesson. And I'm still looking for a curved coffee table to put my curved runner on. The take-home message: Use a walking foot, and don't stretch the binding when you're pinning it to the quilt! (Oh, and wait until you have *good* directions to follow!)

These important pointers are just a taste of the excellent advice, straightforward techniques, and new ideas we've included in this book. It does include good—even excellent— step-by-step directions to help you get over the hump of "I'm done quilting, now what should I do to make this a masterpiece?"

From choosing your finishing method and binding fabric to simple bindings and fancy edge finishes, we've included over a dozen different looks for the edge of your quilt. All with clear step-by-step instructions and photos guaranteed to guide you right through until your quilt is bound, finished, labeled, and hung proudly in your home or at a quilt show.

But a comprehensive book like this one doesn't just come together by itself. With the help of quiltmakers from around the country, this book will show you how to make quilts with professional-looking finished edges. Dixie Haywood and Debra Wagner, favorites on the teaching circuit, knew just what quilters want to see discussed in a book like this. And the team of writers who carried through on their ideas— Mimi Dietrich, Dixie Haywood, Becky Herdle, Susan McKelvey, Ann Seely, Joyce Stewart, Janet Wickell, and Darra Duffy Williamson— provided clear, concise steps that will help you no matter whether you're cutting bias strips, making two-color prairie points, or binding curved edges. You'll also learn all the tricks and tips to tackle binding everything from a miniature to a bed-size quilt.

And when you see the color photos that demonstrate each technique, remember that real quilters made each one of those samples by following the directions in this book.

We have done everything we could to make sure this book is as helpful and accurate as possible. Note that this includes darkening markings and using contrasting thread on some samples so that you can identify them readily in the photos. When we do, we alert you to this at the beginning of the chapter with logos like the ones you see here:

Markings are darkened in these photos for visual clarity.

Thread color contrasts with fabric in these photos for visual clarity.

So, no more excuses! Now you can pick any finishing technique and run right to your sewing machine. Dig through that pile of unbound projects, and get to it! Finish those quilts!

Sarah Sacks Dunn

Sarah Sacks Dunn
Editor

20 Top Tips for *Finishing*

1 Purchased bindings and other edge finishes, such as premade bias binding or cording, can be quick-and-easy ways to finish your quilt. Be sure to choose them carefully, and check that they are the same quality as the quilt fabric. One good product is ReadyBias, which is made from quilting fabric in solids, tone-on-tone prints, and small checks and prints. Call (888) 873-2427 for information or ordering.

2 Always use a sharp rotary blade to trim the edges of your quilt sandwich. A dull blade won't make a clean cut through the layers and may leave a jagged edge.

3 Always use 100 percent cotton thread to sew your binding to quilts made from cotton fabric. Polyester threads, or threads with polyester cores, are stronger than cotton fibers; thus they will eventually cut through the fabric fibers, resulting in a split along the entire binding seam.

4 Sometimes fabric printed off-grain can be a blessing instead of a curse. Straight strips that are cut following the print are often slightly off-grain. This gives the strips some of the same characteristics as bias strips, but with less stretch to contend with during assembly. If the fabric is more attractive when cut off-grain, use it to your advantage.

5 When you fold and press your binding in half for double-fold binding, press it so that the top layer is *slightly* smaller than the bottom layer. When you sew it to the edge of your quilt, you will be able to see both layers and know that you are sewing it precisely to the edge of your quilt without creating small puckers or pleats.

6 As you sew the binding to your quilt, place the binding in your lap. If it hangs off the edge of your sewing table, its own weight can cause it to stretch.

7 Avoid starting and ending your binding in the exact center of a quilt side. Each time you fold your quilt later, it will weaken this spot. Similarly, avoid other potential fold locations—one-quarter of the side and one-third of the length are other frequently folded places.

8 If you are having trouble feeding your layered quilt and binding evenly underneath the presser foot, use a long straight pin or a stiletto to help you ease the binding under the foot. This can be especially helpful as you sew over seams.

9 If you've constructed a pieced binding for your quilt, consider using butted corners rather than mitered ones. This will help you avoid the problem of arranging your binding so no seams fall awkwardly at the mitered corner.

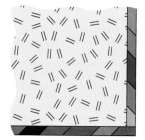

10 If you're having trouble finding binding clips, take a look at your local

pharmacy. Many hair clips have the same spring-action snap-shut feature and can be easily substituted for "real" binding clips.

11 Use large sheets of plain newsprint to design curved and sculptured edges for your quilts. Just fold and cut, creating graceful curved corners with your scissors. When you're satisfied with the edge, transfer the design to the corners and sides of the quilt.

12 To avoid permanent cupping on bound curves, inspect each curve after you bind it. If the curve appears bowed or cupped, clip the stitches, remove the binding, and correct the problem before continuing.

13 If the seams where binding strips are joined are lumpy and bumpy, the problem may be your iron! Check to make sure that you are pressing the seams so that they lie flat. You may want to set the iron on the seam, count to five, then move to the next one. If they still don't lie flat, the problem may be that your iron isn't hot enough. Remember, if your seam allowances bulge, it makes it difficult to sew evenly when attaching the binding to your quilt.

14 When sewing binding to the front of your quilt, use a bobbin thread that is a slightly different color than your backing. Then, when you turn the binding to the back, you'll be able to more easily see your stitching line when you pin the binding in place.

15 For a soft look, cover your fabric cording with voile or another sheer fabric. Construct your cording as you normally would (see page 104), then add the voile over your fabric. The fabric between the cord and the voile adds color impact, but the voile softens the overall effect, creating a more subtle look than if you used the fabric alone.

16 When binding curves, use the steam setting on your iron to coax your bias binding into the right shape. The steam helps loosen the weave just enough to manipulate the binding easily, and the heat from the iron dries the binding and helps it stay in place as you have pressed it.

17 Use leftover fabrics from your quilt top to piece your hanging sleeve. Later, if you need to repair a patch or section of your quilt, the fabrics you will need are right at hand—no need to go searching through your stash!

18 For a permanently attached quilt label, baste or fuse your label into a corner of your quilt *before* you attach the binding. When you bind the quilt, be sure to enclose the two sides of the label at the quilt edges. Those two sides will be permanently sewn onto the quilt back. Hand stitch the other two sides.

Sarah S. Dunn
1998
The Last Hurrah

19 If you want your quilt label to be permanent as well as decorative, consider embroidering your label information directly onto your quilt backing. This is most easily done before you layer the backing and baste and quilt. Use specialty threads and decorative stitches for a fancy look, or simply "write" with a straight stitch.

20 Sign your quilt with both your maiden and married name, if applicable, to aid future genealogists.

Gallery of
Fantastic Finishes

E dge finishes don't have to be an afterthought, that last bit of stitching you do before your quilt is officially done. The quilters whose work is shown in this chapter turned the edges of their quilts into a dynamic design element. We're showcasing these quilts to inspire you to think creatively, add your own special flair, and be bold and daring as you finish off the edges of your quilt.

In Gemstones, quiltmaker Jeanne Jenzano used fabrics from within her quilt to make the multicolor prairie points that frame this stunner. The many colors guide your eye around the quilt and into the center as the colors relate back and forth from the edge to the interior. These prairie points were made using the traditional individual cut-and-fold method; our quick-and-easy strip method is on page 98.

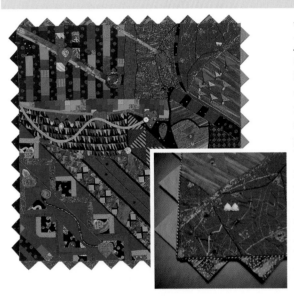

Widely known for her Jacket Jazz, Judy Murrah made this eye-catching quilt using the same techniques she incorporates into her garments. She chose prairie points as a colorful edge finish, varying them on each side. She added a purchased trim to the edge to give it more interest and to repeat the black and gold colors from the interior of the quilt. This quilt even has a musical surprise: Hidden inside the heart at the bottom edge is a small computer chip that plays "London Bridge Is Falling Down!" If you like the look of the black-and-gold cording on this quilt, try it yourself, following the directions on page 104.

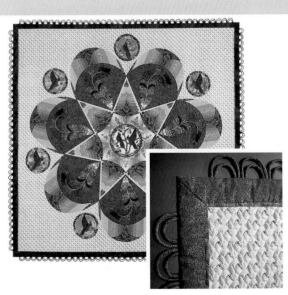

"Wow!" is a typical reaction to June Culvey's award-winning work of art titled Cardinal Virtues. June made each of the nearly 400 loops by wrapping bias strips around 20-inch lengths of nylon macramé yarn. (The macramé yarn is stiff enough to make the loops stand up and away from the quilt.) She then painstakingly positioned and sewed each one in place on the back of the quilt, and then covered the loose ends with an additional facing. If you're inspired to try something similar, follow the steps for the turned-edge finish (see page 85), and insert the loops as you sew the edge closed.

GALLERY OF FANTASTIC FINISHES

11

Double Scallops

Rose Wreath is a mid-1800s antique quilt from the collection of Sara Dillow. The double-scalloped border, which at first glance seems unbelievably intricate, is actually constructed very simply. The borders were cut and appliquéd first, then attached to the quilt top and the backing, then flipped up and away from the quilt. The outer border is twice as wide as the inner border. If you peek in between the borders, you can see the raw edges still there!

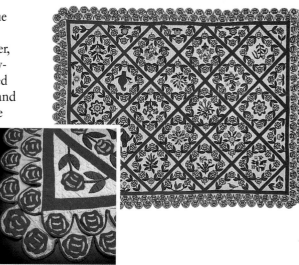

Fringe Flair

Quiltmaker Carla Schwab designed Wool Amish Stars to allow the light-colored hexagons to stand out in the center, then fade away as they head for the sides of the quilt. She backed this table topper with satin and added a shirred cording to the edge. Handmade matching tassels pep up the corners of this very dressy accent piece.

Irregular Edges

Donna Radner's watercolor quilt, Brush Strokes I, mimics trickling water as it hangs on the wall. The wonderful thing about this quilt is that it breaks all the rules: The sides are wavy, the bottom is ragged, and the vertical strip-pieced gradations undulate as if they really were fluid. To finish off the irregular edges, Donna chose to use a hand-finished turned edge. Our instructions for this technique begin on page 85.

Fabric Frenzy

Sometimes, when you're faced with the challenge of choosing which fabric to use to bind your quilt, the best choice is—all of them! Quiltmaker Effie Eschelman pieced together hundreds of scraps to make a binding that echoes the riot of colors and fabrics in her scrappy Charming Hearts. Truly, this quilt is a labor of love!

A Built-In Hanger

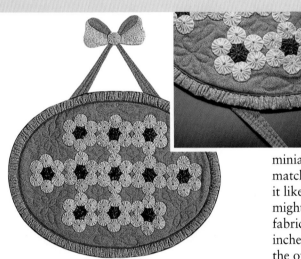

Brown-Eyed Susan is a sweet little wallhanging loaded with fun finishing techniques. Professional quilter Cody Mazuran added decorative piping both inside and outside shirred binding. As an added bonus, she topped off this miniature piece by constructing a matching fabric hanger and treating it like an inserted edge finish (as you might insert prairie points). This fabric confection measures 14½ inches across the widest part of the oval.

Beyond the Binding

Delicate Dresden is another miniature from quilter Cody Mazuran—again with multiple finishing techniques. A corded edge finishes off the sculptured borders of this 18-inch-square wallhanging. Then, for a little added fun, tiny yo-yos adorn the inner curve. Cody carefully cut and positioned each yo-yo—they measure from 1⅛ to 2 inches cut, and finish between ½ and ¾ inch—and then used tiny invisible hand stitches to sew them to each other and to the edge.

Choosing the
Best Binding Method

Pieced and appliquéd, basted and quilted: Time at last to choose how your quilt will be edged. Too often, this important decision is made casually, in the enthusiasm (and fatigue!) of seeing a long-term project near its end. But to treat finishing as an afterthought is to do your labor of love a serious injustice. Instead, think of finishing as one last, wonderful chance to enhance your work and make a statement. Choices abound. Consider them all!

Know Your Choices

There are a number of factors to consider when you're deciding which is the best possible finish for your quilt. Some relate to you: your skill level, your time constraints, your preference for hand or machine work. Some questions involve the finished quilt: How is it quilted? How much use will it receive? How will it be maintained? Too, some considerations are largely practical: Are the quilt's edges straight, irregular, or curved? How much fabric is required? Does the particular method use bias or straight-grain strips? Others are purely aesthetic: What look do you wish to achieve? What mood do you want to create?

The listings that follow in this chapter give you an easy way to scan the options to choose the finishing technique that is the perfect pick for your quilt . . . and for you.

Before you get started, here are a few quick definitions:

An *applied* binding is one that is cut from a separate piece of fabric, then sewn to cover the edges of the quilt.

An *inserted* binding is one that is cut from a separate piece of fabric, then sewn between the layers at the edge of the quilt.

A *self* binding is one in which no separate strips of fabric are added to the edges; the quilt is bound using fabric from the top and/or backing.

Options for Finishing Edges

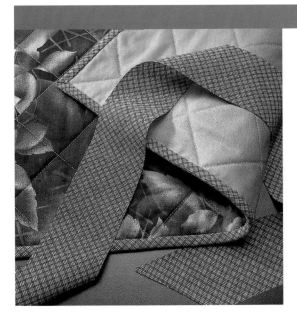

Bias Binding

Description: Binding strips are cut on the bias (at a 45 degree angle to the straight of grain). Bias provides stretchiness, an asset when binding curves or angles. Strips are pieced together to achieve the total length required to bind the project. Can be used for single-fold or double-fold bindings.
Construction method: Applied binding.
Durability: Most durable of all finishes.
Use with: All sizes of quilts and any uses; best finish for curved or angled edges, also works for straight edges; any quilting method and amount.
Special considerations: Usually has more seams than straight-grain binding; handle carefully because it tends to stretch; plaids or stripes make especially attractive bias bindings.
Fabric needs: Requires purchasing additional fabric for binding; uses more fabric than straight-grain binding.
Time commitment: Moderate preparation time; quick to apply.
Overall ease of use: Moderate.

See page 36.

Straight-Grain Binding

Description: Binding strips are cut along the crosswise or lengthwise grain. Strips are sewn together with diagonal seams to achieve the length needed to bind the project. Can be used for single- or double-fold bindings.
Construction method: Applied binding.
Durability: Wears well, though not as durable as bias binding.
Use with: All sizes of quilts and most uses (but *not* baby or crib quilts, since they receive a lot of loving wear); straight edges; any amount or type of quilting.
Special considerations: Straight of grain does not accommodate curves or angles, although cross-grain bindings can adapt to *gentle* curves.
Fabric needs: Requires purchasing additional fabric for binding; strips cut on grain provide economical use of fabric.
Time commitment: Quick to prepare and apply.
Overall ease of use: Easy.

See page 42.

Single-Fold Binding

Description: A single layer of binding is sewn to the quilt edge. The free side of the strip is turned under ¼ inch, then wrapped to the other side of the quilt where it is sewn in place, usually by hand. Can be made with either bias-cut or straight-grain binding.
Construction method: Applied binding.
Durability: Moderate because of the single thickness.
Use with: Small projects that will receive limited use and require little laundering; straight, curved, or angled edges; any quilting method and amount.
Special considerations: A good choice for curves or angles since there's less bulk than with double-fold binding.
Fabric needs: Requires purchasing additional fabric for binding; narrow strips help conserve fabric when cut on straight grain.
Time commitment: Quick to prepare and apply.
Overall ease of use: Easy.

See page 52.

Double-Fold (or French-Fold) Binding

Description: This binding starts with a fabric strip that is folded and pressed in half, wrong sides together. The raw edges are aligned with the edge of the quilt, then stitched in place. The folded binding edge is wrapped to the other side of the quilt, where it is sewn in place, usually by hand. The resulting binding provides a double layer of fabric. Can be made with either bias-cut or straight-grain binding.

Construction method: Applied binding.

Durability: Extremely durable because of the double thickness; bias wears better than straight grain.

Use with: Bed quilts and wallhangings; straight or curved edges; any type and amount of quilting.

Special considerations: Too bulky for smaller projects and miniatures.

Fabric needs: Requires purchasing additional fabric for binding; uses more fabric than single-fold binding.

Time commitment: Quick to prepare and apply.

Overall ease of use: Easy.

See page 56.

Envelope (or Pillowcase) Finish

Description: Before quilting, the layers are basted together inside out. Stitching along the edges holds the layers together; a small opening is left for turning. After the sandwich is turned right side out, the opening is sewn closed by hand and quilting is done.

Construction method: Self binding.

Durability: Not as durable as applied finishes.

Use with: Wallhangings or smaller projects that will receive little wear; straight, curved, and other irregular edges; lightly quilted projects.

Special considerations: Edges are finished before quilt is quilted or tied; requires little hand sewing.

Fabric needs: No additional fabric.

Time commitment: Quick to prepare and sew.

Overall ease of use: Easy.

See page 82.

CHOOSING THE BEST BINDING METHOD

Turned-Edge (or Knife-Edge) Finish

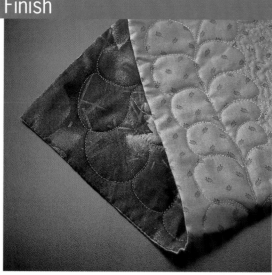

Description: The edges of the quilt top and backing are folded in toward each other ¼ inch each. The perimeter of the quilt is sewn closed, usually with invisible hand stitching.
Construction method: Self binding.
Durability: Not as durable as applied finishes.
Use with: Wallhangings and other smaller projects that will receive minimal wear; straight, curved, or irregular edges; lightly quilted (by hand or machine) or tied projects.
Special considerations: Requires some planning; final ½-inch perimeter must be free of quilting until the edge is finished.
Fabric needs: No additional fabric.
Time commitment: Moderate preparation time; moderate hand sewing time.
Overall ease of use: Easy to intermediate.

See page 82.

Wrapped-Edge Binding

Description: The oversize backing is wrapped to the front, creating a single-thickness, straight-grain edge. The binding is sewn in place either by hand, using invisible stitches, or by machine, using a straight stitch or decorative stitch.
Construction method: Self binding.
Durability: Moderate.
Use with: Wallhangings and other projects that will receive minimal use and laundering; straight edges; lightly quilted (hand or machine) and tied projects.
Special considerations: Remember to oversize backing fabric to allow for wrapping.
Fabric needs: No additional fabric.
Time commitment: Quick to prepare and apply.
Overall ease of use: Easy.

See page 86.

Faced Edge

Description: A single-layer strip of fabric is sewn, right sides together, to the raw edge of the quilt top. The free edge of the facing strip is turned under ¼ inch and then wrapped around to the back of the quilt, where it is sewn in place, usually with invisible hand stitches. Can be made of either bias-cut or straight-grain strips.

Construction method: Applied binding.

Durability: Less durable than traditional binding methods.

Use with: All shapes and sizes of quilts; deep curves or other irregular edges; any quilting method and amount.

Special considerations: Extremely versatile; can be used successfully on quilts with irregular edges.

Fabric needs: Requires purchasing additional fabric for facing; uses more fabric than traditional binding methods.

Time commitment: Preparation can be involved and time-consuming; moderate application time.

Overall ease of use: Intermediate to difficult.

See page 90.

Scalloped Edge

Description: The raw edges of prepared binding are sewn to the quilt top, around the shape of predrawn or precut curves. The binding is then wrapped around to the back of the quilt and sewn in place, usually with invisible hand stitching. Bias-cut binding is recommended.

Construction method: Applied binding.

Durability: As durable as the applied finish used.

Use with: Any size hand or machine quilted project.

Special considerations: Deeper curves are trickier than shallower ones.

Fabric needs: Requires purchasing additional fabric for binding.

Time commitment: Moderately time-consuming and labor intensive.

Overall ease of use: Challenging.

See page 94.

Prairie Points

Description: Folded triangles are added to the edge of the quilt after it is quilted. Usually used in conjunction with a turned-edge finish. The labor-saving continuous prairie point technique uses long fabric strips instead of individual squares to make the triangles.

Construction method: Inserted binding.

Durability: Mainly decorative; less durable than other edge finishes.

Use with: Any size project; most suitable for straight edges; any amount or type of quilting.

Special considerations: Requires some planning to get points to fit; outer ½ inch of quilt must remain unquilted.

Fabric needs: Requires purchasing additional fabric for prairie points; amount varies with size of prairie point desired.

Time commitment: Typically time-consuming and labor intensive; the continuous prairie point technique reduces the time spent cutting and positioning individual triangles.

Overall ease of use: Intermediate.

See page 98.

Piping

Description: A folded strip of fabric added as a decorative accent between the edge of the quilt top and the binding. Can be used with any applied binding method, or with wrapped-edge binding. Uses either bias-cut or straight-grain binding.

Construction method: Used in conjunction with applied and self bindings.

Durability: Decorative element; durability depends on the binding method.

Use with: Any size project (especially dramatic on pillows); any type edge; any type or amount of quilting.

Special considerations: Typically machine sewn.

Fabric needs: Requires purchasing additional fabric for piping.

Time commitment: Preparation and application are time-consuming.

Overall ease of use: Intermediate.

See page 108.

Description: Cording, sometimes called filled piping, is made by covering cable cord with bias binding. Adds a tailored finishing touch to the edge of a quilt.

Construction method: Inserted binding used in conjunction with a turned-edge finish.

Durability: Mainly decorative; less durable than other edge finishes.

Use with: Seen most frequently on pillows and smaller projects, but equally charming on larger quilts; square or rounded corners; any amount or type of quilting.

Special considerations: Normally machine applied; may require a special foot for your sewing machine.

Fabric needs: Requires purchasing additional fabric for binding, as well as cord, yarn, or heavy thread for filler.

Time commitment: Preparation and application are time-consuming.

Overall ease of use: Challenging.

See page 104.

. . . And Beyond

But the possibilities don't end here. There are as many ways to finish the edges of a quilt as a roomful of quilters can imagine. We've included photos of a few extraordinary edge treatments in our "Gallery of Fantastic Finishes," beginning on page 10. Take a look, and be inspired by what other creative quilters have come up with to finish off their quilts.

CHOOSING THE BEST BINDING METHOD

Choosing Fabric
for Your Binding

Last but not *least! That's how you should view the binding on your quilt. It's your final opportunity to make a statement in your quilt's design. Depending on your choice of fabric, you can make the binding shout, hum quietly, or whisper. Choosing the binding for your quilt involves playing with an enormous array of available colors and fabrics. While you're making your selection, remember these three important rules: This is subjective (there's no wrong choice)! This is design! This is fun!*

Getting Ready

You may have been thinking about the binding for your quilt for a while (especially if you sat for hours hand quilting). Perhaps you already know what fabric you want to use; maybe you're waiting for inspiration to strike. Even if you have a general idea, it's fun to audition different fabrics. To make it easy to view your binding selections against the quilt, find a place where you can spread out. For the best preview, spread out the entire quilt on the floor, on a bed, or on a wall. Position the binding fabrics so the equivalent of the binding width sticks out. Be sure to check how a binding fabric looks at a distance. A reducing glass or a pair of binoculars used from the opposite end can give you a good distance view even in tight quarters.

Quilt, quilted and ready for binding

A place to spread out the quilt (a bed or a wall)

Assortment of possible binding fabrics

Assortment of fabrics used in the quilt

Choosing the Best Binding

Think about Color

Use the quilt as a "color road map." Many bindings successfully echo a color within the quilt. Lay your unbound quilt out on a bed and examine it, looking at color only. Squint to blur the lines, and ask yourself these questions: *What colors pop out?* To enhance a particular color or group of colors, repeat them in the binding. *Which color dominates?* To downplay a strong color, avoid using it in the binding. *Is there any color you need more of?* Add it in the binding. *What is the overall color feeling of the quilt?* Echo it by choosing a binding fabric with the same feel.

Play with Fabrics

Audition different binding fabrics.
Fold back the excess backing and
batting along the edge of the quilt.
Place different binding fabrics under
the quilt so only a narrow strip
shows from the front (approximately
as wide as the desired binding). Step
back and see which one you like. Try
folding the same fabric lengthwise,
crosswise, and on the bias to see the
different looks it can create. For inspiration on how to use different fabrics for delightful binding effects, take
a look at the photos that follow.

Match the Border

**Use the same fabric in both border
and binding for an "invisible binding"
effect.** The traditional—and the
simplest—way to bind a quilt is to
use the same fabric as in the outer
border. This is a "safe" method
because it adds no contrast. From a
distance, the binding
appears to be one with
the outer edge and
does not interfere with
the pattern and color
of the quilt.

Change the Pattern

**Duplicate the border fabric color, but
feature a different print.** If you choose
to bind your quilt in the same color
scheme that's used in the border, you
can add a little interest with minimal
risk by using a different pattern or
print. This will add just a touch of
close-up variety while
still appearing as one
color from far away.

Pick Up a Color

For a subtle change, echo a color from *within* the quilt. Because the eye follows color, binding is a perfect place to repeat a color you think is too weak. This repetition has the magical effect of either emphasizing or diluting colors. Echoing also makes the binding a unified part of your quilt, rather than just an afterthought. When echoing, consider the color, not the print, of the binding fabric—it should look the same or very similar in color from a distance.

Vary the Scale of Pattern

Use opposites to attract by contrasting the scale of your binding fabric with what's in the quilt. A big, bold plaid binding contrasts beautifully with a small check border. A quilt with riotous prints benefits from a regularly repeating small-scale print binding. A tiny check, cut on the bias, adds a geometric touch to a floral print border. And a quilt made of geometric prints gets a kick from a binding with big, colorful swirls. Learn to read the patterns in fabrics, then play with the opposite look in your binding.

Try a Large Multicolor Print

Large prints with lots of different colors make exciting bindings. They create movement because within any narrow strip of a large print fabric, the color and design is constantly changing. In addition, they provide a way to get lots of colors into the binding. A large print creates a softer, looser look in the binding. Keep in mind, though, that the unevenness of the pattern creates an irregular line and a less precise edge of color.

Use a Jazzy Stripe

Bindings made of stripes are instant energizers. Cut on the bias, the lines of the stripe run diagonally, making the binding twirl around the quilt's edge like a barber pole. A straight-grain stripe looks great, too, but requires accurate cutting, folding, and sewing. A stripe running parallel to the edge frames the quilt and provides movement, whereas a stripe that runs perpendicular to the edge can create a fringelike effect.

Tip

For a perfectly cut stripe on the bias, use a ruler with a 45 degree angle line, and line it up with one of the lines on the stripe.

Add Movement with Checks

Checks are perfect for bindings. Checks (and plaids), like stripes, create movement and add a nice touch of detailing at the edge of the quilt. Choose a fabric that echoes the colors in the quilt for an understated binding that still has a visual punch. To use a check or plaid in a straight-grain binding, cut it carefully following the lines in the pattern, *not* the grain. Some checks and plaids are printed or woven off-grain, which creates a binding that looks askew when you cut following the grain.

Give a Plaid a Twist

Plaids are also very effective cut on the bias. If you have a plaid border on your quilt, consider using the same plaid in the binding—but cut it on the bias. The color doesn't change, but the binding contrasts gently with its border.

Don't hesitate to use a bias-cut plaid on a quilt that doesn't have any plaid in it. The diagonal lines of the plaid add a dynamic accent that frames the quilt nicely.

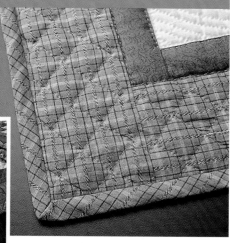

Look for Hidden Stripes

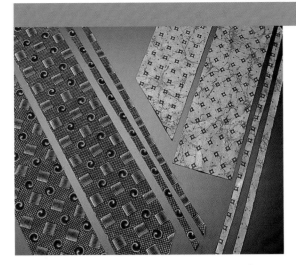

Watch for the change in pattern that emerges on the bias. Many allover prints actually contain stripes. The tan and the blue prints shown here make fine bindings cut on the straight of grain. When cut on the bias, they transform into regularly repeated stripes. Look for prints like these and be aware of the dual opportunity they offer, as well as the multiple patterns available once they're reduced to ¼ inch of visible fabric.

Go to Pieces

For a special effect, create your own binding by piecing fabrics together. This was done for the Color Wheel quilt shown here. Using scraps from all of the bright colors used in the color wheel, this binding becomes an integral part of the quilt design because it echoes all of the brilliant colors of the center.

A pieced binding doesn't have to match the quilt exactly to be eye-catching. **Strips of fabric, cut straight or on an angle, add the same shot of energy a striped fabric does.** By piecing your own binding, you can control the colors and widths of the "stripes."

Let the Color Flow

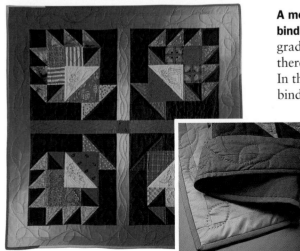

A modulated print makes a wonderful binding. A print that changes colors gradually is basically a stripe and, therefore, has movement built into it. In this quilt, both the border and the binding are made from the same gently modulated print, providing subtle movement around the edge of the quilt. More and more of these kinds of fabrics are appearing on the shelves of quilt shops; play with the exciting design opportunities they provide for attractive bindings.

CHOOSING FABRIC FOR YOUR BINDING

All about
Binding

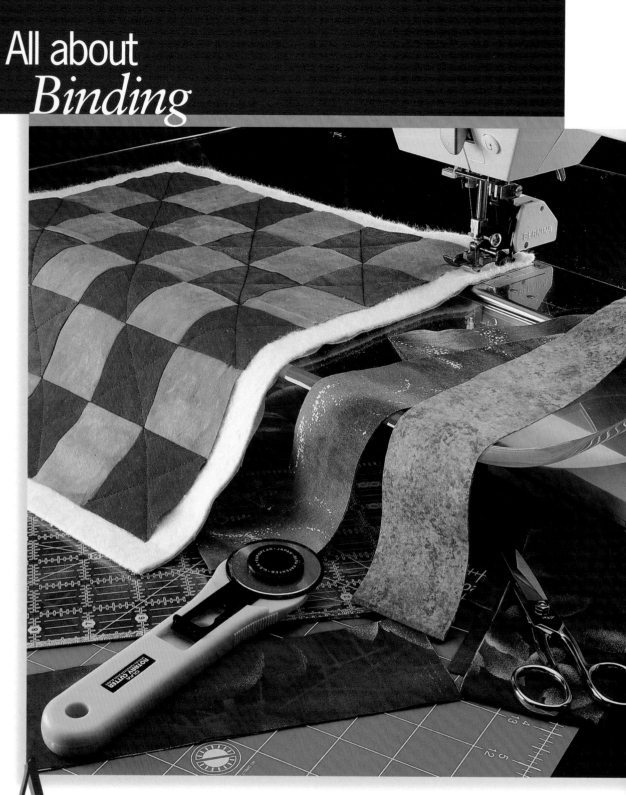

After you determine your ideal binding method and find the perfect binding fabric, you're halfway home. Our step-by-step instructions will walk you through the process of getting your quilt ready for binding and your binding ready to apply to the quilt. We've also included concise, easy-to-use charts that practically guarantee you'll never have to use a calculator again to get your "fantastic finish."

Getting Ready

Before attaching the binding, you must first check to make sure that all sides of the quilt are straight and that the corners are perfectly square. During hand and machine quilting, sides may pull in or corners flare out. Attaching binding to uneven edges doesn't make the problem go away—it just gives you a finished quilt with warped corners and wavy edges. The steps that follow show you how to check for distortion and mark a straight quilt edge that you will use for attaching the binding. To get your quilt ready, remove all basting stitches, pins, and markings. Do not trim the batting and the backing until after the binding has been added (unless specified otherwise in some special binding techniques). Spread the quilt on a large, flat surface and smooth it gently until it is flat.

 Thread color contrasts with fabric in these photos for visual clarity.

Preparing the Quilt

1

Check the sides and corners of your quilt to make sure they are straight. Beginning in an upper corner, **line up the two sides of a large square ruler with the edges of the quilt top.** Use the outermost seam (typically where the border is attached) as an additional alignment guide as you position the ruler. **Mark any areas where the edge of the quilt top is not straight.** Mark as far out from the corner as your ruler reaches on each side. This marked guideline may appear on your quilt top or on the batting, depending on whether the quilt has pulled in or flared out.

Tip

If there's a discrepancy between the edge of the quilt and the outermost seam, use the sewn seam as the positioning guide for the ruler.

2

For quilts without borders, use the blocks as guidelines for marking your straight quilt edge. **If the outermost blocks have points at the edge, line up the ¼-inch lines on the ruler with the tips of the points.**

For blocks without points, measure over from the outermost seam in the block. Place the line on the ruler that equals the finished size of the outermost patch plus ¼ inch for the seam allowance. Here, these blocks are made of 2-inch patches, so the 2¼-inch line is aligned with the seam.

3

Right-handed quilters usually find it easier to work from left to right around the edge; lefties usually work from right to left.

Use a long acrylic ruler to continue marking your straight quilt edge, again lining the ruler up with the last sewn seam. Overlap your previous line by at least 6 inches. As you get within 12 to 15 inches of the next corner, rotate the quilt one-quarter turn so the next corner is at the top (or move yourself around the quilt, whichever is easier). Switch to the square ruler to check for a square corner. Continue in the same manner around the entire quilt, using the square ruler for the corners and the straight ruler for the sides.

4

For an extremely stable edge, stitch a preshrunk ⅛-inch-wide satin ribbon exactly along the straight quilt edge, and enclose it in the finished binding.

Stitch a row of machine basting around the edge of the quilt to prevent shifting and puckering as you attach the binding. Set the stitch length for slightly longer than normal, about 8 stitches per inch. **Using a walking foot attachment or even feed feature, stitch just inside the straight quilt edge** (the edge of the quilt top and/or your drawn line). To keep the basting stable, pivot and turn the corners without lifting the needle.

Preparing the Binding

To help you decide what type of binding you'll use, refer to "Choosing the Best Binding Method" on page 14.

Determine the total length of binding you need for your quilt. **Measure all four sides of your quilt, then add 12 inches** to allow for seams, turning corners, and joining the beginning and ending tails.

Tip

If your quilt has curved or other shaped edges, follow the edge with a piece of string, then measure the string to calculate the length.

Decide how wide you want the finished binding to be. The most frequently used width is approximately ¼ inch. Consider a wider binding if you want the binding fabric to make more of a statement in the overall quilt design. "The Quilter's Problem Solver" on page 34 has charts to help you with the cut width you'll need for your finished binding. Also, you'll find charts to help you with the yardage you'll need to make the amount of binding your quilt requires.

Tip

If you have binding fabric and know the length of binding you need, use the chart on page 34 to find the maximum width your binding strips can be.

To join straight-grain strips into one long binding strip, **position the strips perpendicular to one another, with right sides together.** The end of each strip should overlap the other by at least ¼ inch.

Tip

To keep seams angled in the same direction on the entire length of binding, always place the vertical strip on top, pointing down, when pinning.

ALL ABOUT BINDING

4

Mark a diagonal line on the top strip, from overlap point to overlap point. Use a small square ruler to line up the exact sewing line by placing the 45 degree angle line along one edge of a strip. Pin the strips across the drawn line.

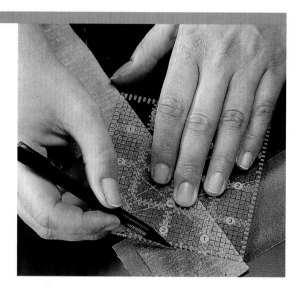

5

Tip

If you're making a quilt that will receive a lot of wear, like a baby quilt, press the seams to the side for extra strength.

Sew the strips together along the drawn line. **Remove them from the sewing machine and use a pair of fabric scissors to trim the seam allowance to ¼ inch.** Press the seam open to distribute the bulk evenly.

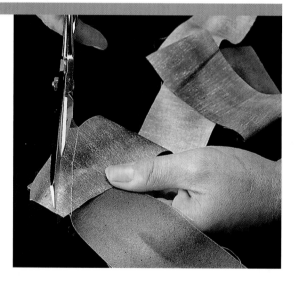

6

Bias-cut strips will already have ends that are at 45 degree angles. To join these into one long binding strip, **position the strips with right sides together, so they form an inverted V. Slide them toward each other until the tips extend ¼ inch beyond the cut edge.** Pin the strips in place, positioning the pins perpendicular to the cut (bias) ends of the strips.

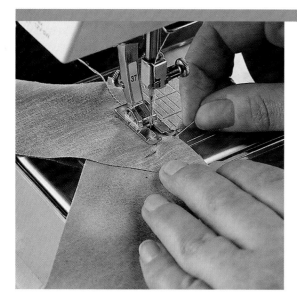

Sew the strips together with a ¼-inch seam. Press the seam open and trim the dog ears (the tiny triangles of fabric that hang over the long edges of the binding) with a pair of fabric scissors.

Hold the pin heads to guide the bias edges under the presser foot, and avoid pulling and distorting the seam.

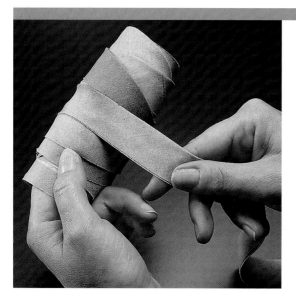

Roll the binding carefully to prevent it from stretching and to make the long strips easier to handle. Refer to "Making and Attaching Single-Fold Binding" on page 52 and "Making and Attaching Double-Fold Binding" on page 56 to prepare your binding for attaching to the quilt. **Then roll it carefully onto an empty cardboard paper towel or bathroom tissue roll.** Use a pin to secure the binding to the roll until you are ready to sew the binding to the quilt.

Before you sew the binding in place, check that no seams will fall at the corners or in other awkward spots. To "preview" the binding on your quilt, begin in the middle of one side, as if you were about to pin and sew the binding in place. **Unroll the binding and lay it out along the edges of the quilt, aligning the raw edges, and turning the corners as you plan to sew them.** If a seam lands on a corner or other problem spot, shift the binding a few inches in either direction.

ALL ABOUT BINDING

The Quilter's
Problem Solver

Taking the Math Out of Binding

Problem	Solution
There's too much math involved in figuring out my binding! Help!	Follow the steps below, and you'll never have to use a calculator again to figure out binding. 1. Refer to "Choosing the Best Binding Method" on page 14 to help decide what type of binding you will use. 2. Refer to Step 2 on page 31 to help decide what width binding you want on your quilt. 3. Refer to Step 1 on page 31 to calculate the length of binding you need to bind the quilt. 4. Find the chart on these pages that best describes your binding needs, and use the information from Steps 1 through 3 above to find the yardage for your binding.
I have the perfect fabric for my binding. How do I know if I have enough?	1. Measure the piece of fabric you want to use for the binding. 2. Refer to Step 1 on page 31 to calculate the length of binding you need to prepare for your quilt. 3. Use the straight-grain and bias charts on the opposite page, along with the numbers you came up with in Steps 1 and 2 above, to find the type and width of binding you can get out of that piece of fabric. Find the amount (yardage) of your fabric piece within the length column of the chart. Then read over to see which width row you land in.

I know how wide I want my binding to look; how wide should I cut it?

Finished measurement (inches)	Cut width (inches) for Single-fold	Cut width (inches) for Double-fold
¼	1	1½
⅜	1½	2
½	2	2½
⅝	2½	3
¾	3	3½
1	4	4½
1½	6	6½
2	8	8½

I know my binding width and length. How many yards will I need for straight-grain binding?

Cut width of binding (inches)	Yardage* needed if your binding length (inches) is				
	Up to 150	150–200	200–350	350–450	450–500
1	¼	¼	⅓	⅜	½
1½	¼	⅓	½	⅝	⅝
2	⅓	⅓	⅝	¾	⅞
2½	⅓	½	¾	1	1
3	⅜	½	⅞	1⅛	1¼
3½	½	⅝	1	1¼	1⅓
4	½	⅝	1⅛	1½	1½
4½	⅝	⅔	1¼	1⅝	1¾
5	⅝	¾	1⅓	1¾	1⅞
5½	⅔	⅞	1½	2	2⅛
6	¾	1	1⅝	2⅛	2¼
6½	⅞	1	1¾	2¼	2½
7	⅞	1⅛	1⅞	2½	2⅝
7½	1	1⅛	2	2⅝	2⅞
8	1	1¼	2⅛	2¾	3
8½	1	1¼	2¼	3	3⅛

*Based on crosswise strips cut from 40"-wide fabric after shrinking.

I know my binding width and length. How many yards of fabric will I need for bias-cut binding?

Cut width of binding (inches)	Yardage* needed if your binding length (inches) is		
	Up to 200	200–350	350–500
1	½	⅝	¾
1½	⅝	¾	⅞
2	⅝	⅞	1
2½	¾	⅞	1⅛
3	¾	1	1⅛
3½	⅞	1	1¼
4	⅞	1⅛	1⅜
4½	⅞	1⅛	1⅜
5	1	1¼	1½
5½	1	1¼	1½
6	1	1⅜	1⅝
6½	1⅛	1⅜	1⅝
7	1⅛	1½	1¾
7½	1⅛	1½	1¾
8	1¼	1½	1⅞
8½	1¼	1⅝	1⅞

*Based on 40"-wide fabric after shrinking. Use the square method on page 37. Cut the largest square possible from your fabric.

All the Basics on
Bias Binding

Nothing beats bias binding for versatility and durability. Equally at home on curves and corners, this nifty edging lasts longer and wears better than any of its rival finishes. If you've considered bias labor-intensive and hard to handle, read on. Our easy instructions and time-saving tips minimize the pitfalls and maximize the advantages.

Getting Ready

Bias-cut strips of fabric are cut at a 45 degree angle to the grain (weave) of the fabric. This gives them lots of stretch, making them perfect for handling curved edges. This chapter describes two ways to make bias binding: cutting and joining individual strips, and constructing a continuous length of binding. Here is a comparison of their characteristics:

Bias Strips
Strips are cut and sewn together individually
Many seams
Simple to cut and join strips

Continuous Bias
Cut one long strip, already seamed
Fewer seams
Somewhat tricky to construct and cut

 Thread color contrasts with fabric and markings are darkened in these photos for visual clarity.

What You'll Need

Quilt, quilted and ready for binding

Prewashed, pressed cotton fabric for binding

Thread to match binding

Rotary cutter, mat, and 6" × 24" acrylic ruler

Acrylic ruler with 45 degree marking or edge

Pencil

Fabric scissors

Silk pins

Sewing machine

Walking foot attachment or even feed feature

Hand sewing needles

Thread snips

Iron and ironing board

Individual Bias Strips

To cut and assemble individual bias strips, start with a prewashed, pressed square of fabric. Refer to page 35 to decide how big a square you will need.

Fold the fabric square in half diagonally on the true bias to form a 45 degree angle. **Check the accuracy of the fold with the 45 degree side of a triangle,** or with an acrylic ruler with a 45 degree marking. **Fold the fabric triangle a second time** to bring the top corner down to meet the bottom corner. Once again, check the accuracy of the angle with a triangle or ruler.

Tip
If you are using a stripe or plaid, cut the square either along or perpendicular to the *print*, not the grain.

2

Before you can cut bias strips, you need to cut the fold off the triangle. **Align a line on a 24-inch acrylic ruler with the double-folded edge of the square, positioning the edge of the ruler about ⅛ inch from the fold. Trim off the folded edge.**

3

Determine the width you want your binding strips. **Use a rotary cutter, mat, and ruler to cut the fabric into strips the size you need** (the ones shown here are 2 inches wide). Unfold the strips to prepare for sewing.

4

Tip

If the tips of your strips don't align as shown, use the opposite end of one strip.

Sew the strips together on the diagonal as described on page 32. To minimize the number of seams, start with the longest strips and progress to the shorter ones as needed to reach the desired binding strip length. **Trim the seams to a scant ¼ inch, press them open, and trim off the dog ears** (the tiny protruding triangle tips). When you have the needed length, prepare binding as described in "Making and Attaching Single-Fold Binding" on page 52 and "Making and Attaching Double-Fold Binding" on page 56.

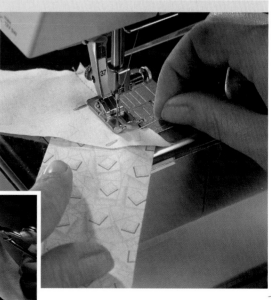

Continuous Bias Binding

To make a continuous length of bias binding, find the size square required for the amount of binding you need on page 35. **Cut the appropriately sized square, and fold it in half diagonally in each direction.** Press the folds, taking care not to stretch or otherwise distort the fabric.

Open the fabric square and cut it apart corner to corner, along *one* diagonal fold line. Label the corners *not* cut A and B.

Tip

To calculate your square size yourself, multiply the length of binding needed by the width of the binding strip, then take the square root of that number.

Place the two triangles right sides together so that they overlap along one short side. Point A should be on one end and Point B on the other. Pin, then sew the two triangles together from A to B, using a scant ¼-inch seam. Unpin and unfold the sewn triangles, and **press the seam open.**

Tip

When preparing to work with bias edges, you may find fabric easier to handle if you first apply a light coat of spray starch.

Position the sewn triangle unit with the wrong side (seam side) up. Use a pencil and ruler to mark a line parallel to one bias edge of the sewn unit. The width of the marked strip should equal the desired cut width of the bias binding. **Continue marking parallel lines equal to the cut width of the binding until you have reached the opposite bias edge.**

Tip

Trim off the excess fabric beyond the last marked line.

ALL THE BASICS ON BIAS BINDING

Tip

Draw the ¼-inch seam line on both straight edges to use as a guide to help the lines intersect exactly.

4

Turn the sewn unit over so the wrong side faces down. Fold the triangle tips in toward each other; the marked lines should be visible. **Align the diagonal edges, then offset the sides of the tube so that the beginning of one edge aligns with the first marked line of the other at the seam line.**

When you are sure that the lines are properly positioned, pin, then sew the two edges together, taking a scant ¼-inch seam.

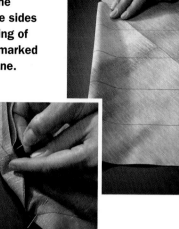

5

Check to see that your drawn lines meet. Lay the binding tube out and check that the lines appear to run continuously. Flip the seam allowance out of the way as you check each side. If necessary, rip out and resew the seam, repositioning the edges. When the seam has been sewn to your satisfaction, press it open.

6

Tip

A 6 × 9-inch cutting mat will fit easily inside a tube made from an 18-inch square.

The easiest way to cut the tube into a binding strip is to use a rotary cutter, mat, and ruler. Place the mat on your ironing board. **Slide the tube over the board and position the end where you will cut on top of the mat.** Cut along the continuous drawn line, rotating the tube around the ironing board and mat until you come to the end.

Prepare the binding for single-fold or double-fold binding as described in "Making and Attaching Single-Fold Binding" on page 52 and "Making and Attaching Double-Fold Binding" on page 56.

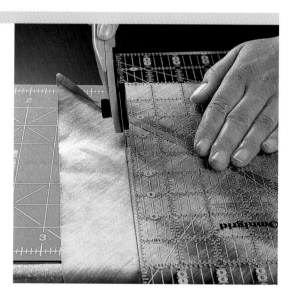

The Quilter's
Problem Solver

Manipulating the Bias Tube

Problem	Solution
It is difficult to keep the fabric tube "un- tangled" when working with it.	When the tube becomes unruly, place your hands inside it, and open it up a little so that it forms an oval. Smooth it flat with your hands; spray it lightly with spray starch; then press it lightly, staying away from the folds.
The tube won't fit over the end of the ironing board when it's time to cut it into a binding strip.	Simply use fabric scissors to cut carefully along the drawn line.

Skill Builder

Keep these tips in mind for trouble-free bias binding:

❏ Use a dry iron and an up-and-down (*not* back-and-forth) motion when pressing bias folds and strips.

❏ This is not the time to skimp on pins! Stabilize the binding before stitching it to the quilt by pinning generously.

❏ Don't pull or tug on the binding when applying it to the quilt. Remember that bias s-t-r-e-t-c-h-e-s and can easily be-come distorted. The even feed feature or walking foot attach-ment of your sewing machine can be a tremendous help.

Try This!

Minimize the number of seams in bias binding by starting with a larger piece of fabric. Instead of 36 inches, cut a square with sides equal to the full width of the fabric—typically 42 to 44 inches. The resulting strips will be longer, so you'll need to cut fewer strips and sew fewer seams! Leftovers can be used to cut other pieces for the quilt. Try a larger square for the continuous bias method, too. The seams will be more generously spaced.

All about
Straight-Grain Binding

S traight-grain binding might easily be called the workhorse of finishing techniques. Its crisp appearance, economical use of fabric, ease of handling, and simple application make it the perfect choice for myriad straight-edged quilting projects. This simple, step-by-step approach to planning and cutting virtually guarantees success!

Getting Ready

Fabric has two types of woven threads (or grain): *crosswise* (which run from selvage to selvage) and *lengthwise* (which run from cut edge to cut edge off the bolt).

Typically, crosswise threads do not run perfectly straight across the fabric. Binding strips cut crosswise have a slight stretch. When the binding is turned over the edge of a quilt, multiple crosswise threads fall along this edge, giving it extra durability.

The threads of lengthwise grain run perfectly parallel to the selvage, giving lengthwise binding very little stretch. A single thread will run along the turned edge of a binding, making the binding more vulnerable to wear and tear.

Fabrics are not always printed exactly on grain, so you may have to cut along the pattern instead, especially when working with stripes or plaids.

Cutting Crosswise Strips

Binding strips cut on the crosswise grain can be quite economical, yielding a large number of strips from a relatively modest amount of yardage. To cut crosswise strips, fold your fabric selvage to selvage on a large cutting mat. Align the selvages exactly and smooth the fold. **Align the 1-inch line on a 24-inch acrylic ruler with the fold, and make a cut along the length of the ruler to square up one side.** (Righties will square up the right side; lefties will square up the left side.)

Tip

To determine a fabric's grain line, grasp the fabric in two hands, tug and listen. Lengthwise grain will "snap," whereas crosswise grain will "thud."

2

Turn the cutting mat 180 degrees, and align the ruler with the square edge. **Match the line that corresponds to the desired cut width of binding strips with the straight edge of the fabric.** Cut the required number of binding strips. (Righties will cut from the left side; lefties, from the right side.) Resquare the edge of your fabric every 6 inches or so to make sure you're cutting perfectly straight strips.

Cutting Lengthwise Strips

1

Lengthwise binding strips are trickier to cut because they are usually longer than your ruler and mat. Fold the fabric in half, selvage to selvage, and square up both cut ends. Then fold in half again, cut edge to cut edge. (You will have four layers of fabric.) **Place the folded fabric on a large cutting mat with the single fold toward you and the double fold to your left** (lefties should place the double fold to their right). Square up one vertical edge along the length of your ruler.

2

To finish squaring up the edge, slide the ruler up the fabric. If the fabric is hanging off the cutting mat, carefully hold the fabric in place and slide the mat underneath the fabric so you can continue the cut. **Line up about 5 inches of the ruler with the previous cut, and continue your squaring-up cut.** Continue sliding the ruler and the mat until you have squared up the entire edge.

To cut your lengthwise binding strips, position your squared-up edge to your left (lefties to the right) and **line up the appropriate line on your ruler with the square edge to cut the width strip you need.** Follow the instructions in Step 2 at the bottom on the opposite page to slide the ruler and mat to cut strips the length of the fabric.

Working with Skewed Fabric

Most fabrics are printed straight along the lengthwise grain. However, some patterns become distorted slightly on the crosswise grain, either during manufacturing or laundering. If you are cutting crosswise binding strips, **check first to make sure the pattern runs perpendicular to the fold by lining the ruler up with a fold and visually checking the pattern.**

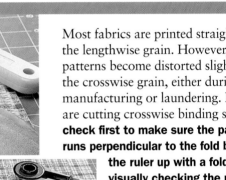

If the pattern is skewed, unfold the fabric and cut just one layer of fabric at a time. **Align your ruler with a line on the fabric** and cut strips straight along the pattern line.

It is possible to straighten skewed fabric, as long as it is no more than 3 inches off grain. **Make a small snip into the selvage, then tear straight across the piece of fabric along the crosswise grain at each end of the fabric.** This torn edge indicates the straight of grain.

Then, with a helper, **grasp opposite sides of the fabric along the selvage, holding it so that you pull firmly at a 45 degree angle to the torn edge** until the torn end is as square as possible to the selvages. Move along the selvages about 8 inches at a time, until you have squared the entire length of the piece.

The Best Methods for
Joining Binding Ends

S ewing the binding to the quilt isn't the hard part—it's how to connect the start and the
end of the binding strip so you end up with a smooth, flat seam that doesn't call attention to itself. Here are the two best ways to camouflage your starting and ending point
with minimum fuss and maximum finesse.

Getting Ready

This chapter details two very successful methods for joining the ends of your binding: the diagonal seam and the tuck. Both techniques produce a professional-looking binding, and both make a smooth, unobtrusive joining place along the edge of your quilt. The diagonal seam method can be used with both single-fold and double-fold bindings. The tuck method is just a little quicker, but can be used only with double-fold binding.

Refer to "All about Binding" on page 28, "Making and Attaching Single-Fold Binding" on page 52, and "Making and Attaching Double-Fold Binding" on page 56 for instructions on making and attaching binding.

Thread color contrasts with fabric in these photos for visual clarity.

What You'll Need

Quilt, quilted and ready for binding

Prepared binding

Thread to match binding

Fabric scissors

Silk pins

Sewing machine

Walking foot attachment or even feed feature

Iron and ironing board

Diagonal Seam Method

The following photos feature mainly double-fold binding, but this method can also be used successfully for single-fold binding. Key steps for single-fold binding are shown and labeled in the smaller inset photos.

Trim the ends of the binding at a 45 degree angle to match the direction of the diagonal seams used to join the strips. Beginning in the middle of one side of the quilt, line up the raw edges of the binding with the straight quilt edge. **Start sewing 3 inches from the end of the binding, using a ¼-inch seam.** The portion of the binding you leave free is called the *starting tail* in the rest of these directions.

Tip

A walking foot attachment or even feed feature is one of the best ways to ensure pucker-free binding.

JOINING BINDING ENDS

2

Sew the binding to the quilt top, aligning the raw edges of the binding with the straight quilt edge. **Hold the binding in position with your hands, stopping to adjust the alignment about every 4 inches.** Refer to "Mastering Miters" on page 62 for directions on handling the corners. Stop sewing about 8 inches from the place you started sewing the binding to the quilt. **Trim the binding strip, leaving a 12-inch tail.** This portion of the binding is called the *ending tail* in the rest of these directions.

Tip

If your machine has a needle-down setting, use it while turning corners and pausing to line up the binding.

3

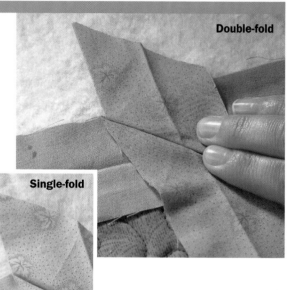

Double-fold

Single-fold

Unfold both tails on the binding. (For single-fold binding, unfold the ¼ inch you pressed under previously.) **Fold the starting tail up at a 90 degree angle and the ending tail down at a 90 degree angle, keeping the folds butted against each other.** You should see the right side of the fabric of each tail going vertically. Temporarily refold the binding in half lengthwise and check that the seam angles in the same direction as the other seams in the binding. If not, trade directions so that the tail that pointed up now points down, and vice versa. Finger press a crease in each strip.

Tip

Use the handle of your scissors to gently press a crisp crease on the tails.

4

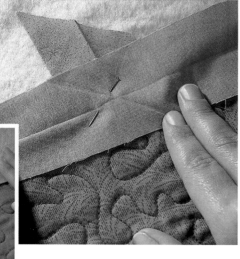

Unfold the ending tail and lay it over the starting tail, right sides together, lining up the creases. **Pin across the crease; then sew along the crease line.** Remove the pin, and **check to see that the binding fits smoothly against the quilt.** If no adjustments are needed, trim the seam allowance to ¼ inch and press the seam open.

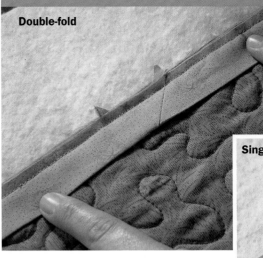

Double-fold

Single-fold

Refold the binding. Line up the raw edges of the binding with the straight quilt edge. **Sew the binding to the quilt top, overlapping the previous stitching by about 1 inch on each end.**

Tuck Method

1

This method works with double-fold binding only.

To begin, create an angle on the starting tail by first unfolding the binding strip. With the wrong side of the binding fabric facing up, **fold down the left corner diagonally, and press a crease along the fold. Using scissors, trim off the corner ¼ inch outside the fold.**

Tip

Make sure the angle on your starting tail matches the photo. If not, square the end, fold, and trim again.

2

With the strip still unfolded, begin in the middle of one side of your quilt and align the raw edge of the binding with your straight quilt edge. **Using a walking foot attachment or even feed feature, begin sewing from the end of the binding, using a ¼-inch seam.** Stitch through the single thickness of binding for about 4 inches.

Tip

Make sure you're lining up and sewing along the longer edge of the binding.

3

Lift the presser foot and remove the quilt from the machine. Refold the binding. **Leave about 1 inch unsewn, and resume sewing the binding to the quilt, sewing through both layers of binding.**

Tip

An awl is a handy tool to completely smooth the ending tail in place and hold it there as you finish stitching.

4

Continue sewing the binding to the quilt top, aligning the raw edges of the binding with the straight quilt edge. Hold the binding in position with your hands and stop and adjust the alignment about every 4 inches. Refer to "Mastering Miters" on page 62 for directions on handling the corners. Sew to within 4 inches of your starting point. **Stop with the needle down, and trim off any excess on your ending tail so the strips overlap by about ¾ inch. Tuck the ending tail into the starting tail.**

5

Continue stitching, sewing through all thicknesses. Overlap your beginning stitches by about 1 inch.

The Quilter's
Problem Solver

Problems with Seams

Problem	Solution
Diagonal join doesn't lie flat on the edge of the quilt.	The first rule of joining binding ends "invisibly" is patience, patience, patience. Take your time to smooth all the layers, line up the strips carefully, pin them in place, and check your placement before you sew. If you do all this and still don't get a flat join, take out your stitches and try again. If you're consistently having trouble getting a good invisible join, you may want to try the tuck method instead.
Tucked join is lumpy and bumpy.	Make sure that your ending tail is tucked completely into your starting tail. It must be smooth and flat for the binding to make the turn to the back and leave a smooth finish on the front. If you don't have an awl to help tuck the ending tail, try a small crochet hook or a tiny screwdriver.

JOINING BINDING ENDS

Skill Builder

Disguise the fact that your joining seam isn't perfect.

Just because you aren't the Michelangelo of joining binding ends doesn't mean that you can't make your binding look like a masterpiece anyway. Decorative threads, specialty embellishing items, and your sewing machine can be your best ally here! Try stitching a decorative stitch on the front of your binding, using a specialty thread that will distract all eyes from your problem. Or, use clear monofilament thread to zigzag over a thicker thread or embellishment and similarly decorate your quilt's edge.

Try This!

Finish off your tucked binding ends with invisible hand stitches. To make sure that your binding ends never separate, use tiny blind stitches to sew the joined ends together. Sew as you would for appliqué, picking up only one or two threads at a time, and keeping your stitches very close together. This way, the joined portion of your binding won't separate and fray.

Making and Attaching
Single-Fold Binding

One choice for finishing the edges of your quilt is single-fold binding, which is just what its name implies. A long strip made from a single layer of fabric is sewn to the front side of the quilt; then the unsewn edge is folded under, wrapped to the back of the quilt, and blind stitched to the backing. This is a particularly popular method for binding small quilts, such as doll quilts and miniatures.

Getting Ready

Before you decide to use single-fold binding, determine what type of corner treatment you prefer, and consider how the quilt will be used. Single-fold binding helps reduce corner bulk in quilts with butted, rather than mitered, corners. And it can be a good choice for quilts with scalloped or other curved edges, since a single layer of fabric is easy to manipulate around curves (particularly if you cut the binding along the bias). Single-fold binding is appropriate for miniature quilts and wallhangings, too, because a more delicate binding often enhances the appearance of small projects.

Refer to "Choosing Fabric for Your Binding" on page 22 for help with fabric selection. "All about Binding" on page 28 tells you how to prepare the length of bias or straight-grain binding you need, plus how to prepare your quilt for binding.

Thread color contrasts with fabric in these photos for visual clarity.

What You'll Need

Quilt, quilted and ready for binding

Prepared binding

Thread to match binding

Rotary cutter, mat, and acrylic ruler

Fabric scissors

Silk pins

Sewing machine

Walking foot attachment or even feed feature

Hand sewing needles

Thread snips

Binding clips

Iron and ironing board

Attaching Single-Fold Binding

1

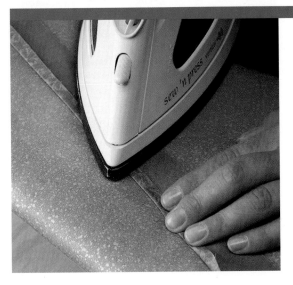

With the wrong side of your binding facing up, turn under and lightly press ¼ inch along one long edge of the entire binding strip. A gentle crease allows you to make corrections to the fold later and is all that's necessary to help you turn under the edge more easily during the final step of applying binding. Use an up-and-down pressing motion; dragging the iron back and forth across the strip can stretch it out of shape.

A ¼-inch bias press bar provides a handy guide for pressing under just the right amount.

SINGLE-FOLD BINDING

Tip

You may prefer to omit pins; hold the binding in place as you sew about 4 inches at a time, pausing to realign as needed.

2

Refer to page 47 for instructions on starting the binding.

Place the binding strip on the quilt top, right sides together, and align the raw (unfolded) edge of the binding with the straight quilt edge. Use silk pins to secure several inches of binding to the quilt.

3

Sew the binding to the quilt with a ¼-inch seam allowance. Remove the pins as you come to them. See "Mastering Miters" on page 62, "Mastering Other Corner Finishes" on page 70, and "Mitering Uncommon Corners" on page 76 to pick a method for handling your corners. Refer to "The Best Methods for Joining Binding Ends" on page 46 for help on ending your binding.

4

Trim the batting and backing to the desired width. **Most quilters will trim the batting and backing even with the straight quilt edge** to produce a ¼-inch binding on the front of the quilt. Simply line your acrylic ruler up with the straight quilt edge, and rotary cut the excess batting and backing from the quilt.

If, however, you have decided on a binding wider than ¼ inch, you will trim your batting and backing wider than the straight quilt edge. **Measure over from the seam line, where you sewed your binding on, an amount equal to your desired finished binding width,** and cut the excess batting and backing off as above.

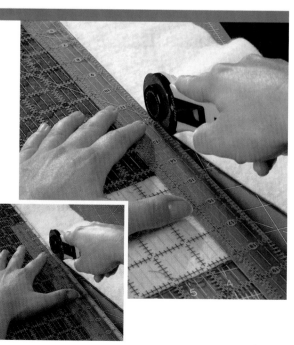

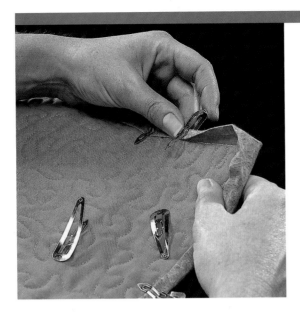

Fold the binding over the layered quilt edge to the quilt back, fitting it snugly over the seam allowance. The fold of the binding should just cover your line of stitches from sewing on the binding. The prepressed fold should turn under easily and provide a finished edge on the back side of the quilt. **Use binding clips (available at quilt shops or in quilt supply catalogs) to secure the binding to the edges of the quilt.** These hold as snugly as silk pins, but without sharp points to prick fingers and snag threads.

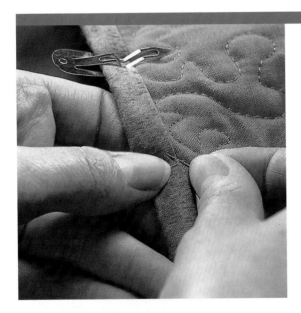

Use matching thread to blind stitch the fold of the binding to the backing. **Pick up just one or two threads of the backing fabric exactly underneath the edge of the binding, then slide your needle into the fold in the binding.** Bring the needle back out of the fold about ⅛ inch away from where you entered. Continue stitching in this manner all the way around the quilt.

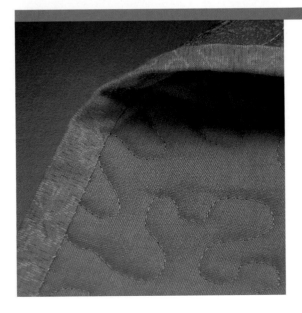

The closer together you make the blind stitches, the more durable your binding will be. For a bed quilt that will be frequently handled and laundered, use smaller, closer stitches. On a wall quilt, you can get away with more generously spaced stitches.

Making and Attaching
Double-Fold Binding

*W*hen you consider its incredible staying power, its snappy good looks, and its chameleon-like versatility, it's no wonder that quiltmakers favor double-fold binding for both everyday and heirloom projects. As an added bonus, the folded edge makes short work of turning and finishing.

Getting Ready

Double-fold (also called French-fold) binding is just what the name implies: binding cut and folded to form two layers. This chapter examines two techniques for attaching and finishing double-fold binding. One method is straightforward and simple: The binding is machine stitched to the front of the quilt, turned to the back, and secured in place with invisible hand stitches.

The second method adds a decorative touch. The binding is machine stitched to the *back* of the quilt, turned, and then secured to the front with novelty threads and fancy machine stitchery. For best results, use butted corners (page 71) with this method.

Refer to "All about Binding" on page 28 for tips on how to prepare the length of bias or straight-grain binding you need, plus how to prepare your quilt for binding.

Thread color contrasts with fabric in these photos for visual clarity.

What You'll Need

Quilt, quilted and ready for binding

Prepared binding

Thread to match binding

Decorative thread (variegated rayon, silk, metallic)

Rotary cutter, mat, and acrylic ruler

Pencil

Fabric scissors

Silk pins

Sewing machine

Walking foot attachment or even feed feature

Special feet as needed for decorative stitching

Hand sewing needles

Thread snips

Binding clips

Iron and ironing board

Attaching Binding from the Front

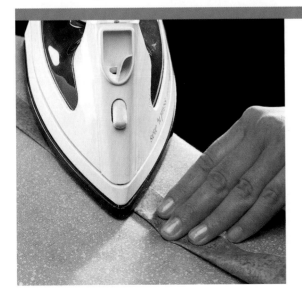

1

Fold the binding strip lengthwise with wrong sides together. Press, lifting the iron in an up-and-down motion. Take extra care not to distort or stretch the fabric, particularly if you have cut the strips on the bias.

Tip

Don't let a long length of bias binding hang over the edge of your ironing board—its weight will stretch it out of shape.

2

Refer to page 46 for instructions on starting the binding.

Place the binding strip on the quilt top, and align the raw edges of the binding with the straight quilt edge. Use silk pins to secure several inches of binding to the quilt.

Tip

Pinning is optional. Hold the binding in place as you sew about 4 inches at a time, pausing to realign as needed.

3

Sew the binding to the quilt with a ¼-inch seam allowance. Remove the pins as you come to them. Handle the corners as described for your preferred method; see pages 62–81. See page 46 for help on how to join the ends of your binding.

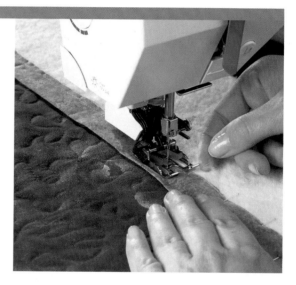

4

Trim the batting and backing to the desired width. **Most quilters trim the batting and backing even with the straight quilt edge** to produce a ¼-inch binding on the front of the quilt. Line up your acrylic ruler with the straight quilt edge, and rotary cut the excess batting and backing from the quilt.

If you have decided on a binding wider than ¼ inch, trim the batting and backing wider than the straight quilt edge. **From the binding seam line, measure over an amount equal to the desired finished binding width,** and cut off the excess batting and backing.

Tip

If your ruler tends to slip while you're cutting, add traction with dots of rubber cement on the underside.

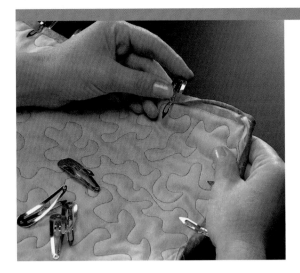

Fold the binding over the layered quilt edge to the quilt back, fitting it snugly over the seam allowance. The fold of the binding should just cover the line of stitches made by sewing on the binding. Use binding clips (available at quilt shops or in quilt supply catalogs) to secure the folded binding along the edges of the quilt. These hold as snugly as silk pins, but without sharp points to prick fingers and snag threads.

Follow the directions in Steps 6 and 7 on page 55 to sew the binding to the back of the quilt.

Attaching Binding from the Back

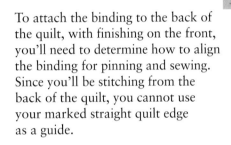

Front

Back

To attach the binding to the back of the quilt, with finishing on the front, you'll need to determine how to align the binding for pinning and sewing. Since you'll be stitching from the back of the quilt, you cannot use your marked straight quilt edge as a guide.

Turn the quilt so that the front is facing you. **Use your sewing machine to sew a long basting stitch through the batting and backing, immediately outside your marked straight quilt edge. When you turn the quilt over, this line of stitching becomes your guideline.**

Prepare your binding as directed in Step 1 on page 57. Align the raw edges of the binding with the basting stitches you sewed in Step 1. The fold of the binding should face toward the center of the quilt. Pin the binding in place if desired. **Use a scant ¼-inch seam allowance and sew the binding to the quilt.** Handle the corners as described on page 71. See page 46 for help on how to join the ends of the binding.

DOUBLE-FOLD BINDING

3

Trim the batting and backing to the desired width. **Most quilters trim the batting and backing even with the straight quilt edge** to produce a ¼-inch binding on the front of the quilt. Line up your acrylic ruler with the straight quilt edge, and rotary cut the excess batting and backing from the quilt.

If you have decided on a binding wider than ¼ inch, trim the batting and backing wider than the straight quilt edge. From the binding seam line, measure over an amount equal to the desired finished binding width, and cut off the excess batting and backing, as shown in Step 4 on page 58.

4

Tip

Remove the clips or pins only immediately before you get to them in this method. It keeps the binding straighter on the front of the quilt.

Fold the binding over the layered quilt edge to the quilt front, fitting it snugly over the seam allowance. The fold of the binding should just cover the line of stitches from sewing on the binding. Use binding clips (available at quilt shops or in quilt supply catalogs) or silk pins to secure the folded binding to the edges of the quilt.

5

Tip

Stitch close to the folded edge of the binding— about ¹⁄₁₆ inch away—so the edge doesn't flip up.

Sew the binding to the front of the quilt. **Use a straight stitch or a decorative stitch, if your machine offers that option.** Use specialty threads like rayon, metallic, or silk if you want to call extra attention to this stitching. Match the bobbin thread to the binding.

The Quilter's
Problem Solver

Stitching Invisibly

Problem	Solution
The hand stitching used to finish bindings shows too prominently.	To keep the stitches of hand-finished bindings invisible, try to: ❏ Master one reliable invisible stitch. The appliqué stitch (thread advanced behind the fabric), the blind hem stitch (thread advanced in the fold), and the ladder stitch (thread advanced behind the fabric *and* in the fold) all achieve fine results. ❏ Match thread to the color of the binding fabric. Use a neutral, such as gray, for multicolored bindings. ❏ Keep stitches as tiny as possible and no farther than ¹⁄₁₆ inch apart. ❏ Pull thread snugly enough so that the stitches are secure, but not so tight as to pucker the binding. ❏ Be sure that stitches do not pierce the front of the quilt.

Skill Builder

Avoid ripples, pleats, and twists in your binding by:

❏ Carefully aligning the raw edges when folding binding strips for pressing.

❏ Pressing gently. Use a dry iron, and an up-and-down—not back-and-forth—motion.

❏ Basting around the edges of the quilt to hold them securely throughout the binding process.

❏ Pinning generously!

❏ Using a walking foot attachment or even feed feature on your sewing machine to guide the layers smoothly under the presser foot.

Try This!

Daunted by the thought of finishing your binding with traditional hand-stitched methods? Totally replace the hand sewing by using a fusible thread such as Thread Fuse in your sewing machine. Substitute fusible thread for cotton in your bobbin, and stitch the binding to your quilt as usual. Turn the binding to the back of the quilt and heat set it in place with an iron. Absolutely no hand sewing required!

Mastering
Miters

Mitering binding corners takes a bit of time and effort, but the payoff is big—
a professional-looking edge finish with crisply defined corners for your quilts.
Quiltmaker and teacher Becky Herdle found the secret to the perfect mitered
corner is taking two key measurements accurately. Following her technique will make your
mitered corners tight and square, no matter how wide your binding strips or seam allowances
are. You'll also learn how to hand sew miters closed perfectly every time—whether you're
a leftie or a rightie!

Getting Ready

Mitered corners are perhaps the most often bemoaned binding technique—but they don't have to be! If you just go slowly and carefully at each step, you'll be assured of flat, even miters on every corner of your quilt.

Your first step should be to square up your quilt (see page 29). Then, prepare bias or straight-grain binding, following the instructions in "All the Basics on Bias Binding" on page 36 or "All about Straight-Grain Binding" on page 42. Double-fold binding is extremely well suited to mitered corners; instructions for preparing it begin on page 57.

▶ *Thread color contrasts with fabric and markings are darkened in these photos for visual clarity.*

What You'll Need

Quilt, quilted and ready for binding

Prepared binding

Thread to match binding

6-inch metal seam gauge

Marking pencil

Silk pins

Sewing machine

Walking foot attachment or even feed feature

Hand sewing needles

Thread snips

Machine Stitching Miters

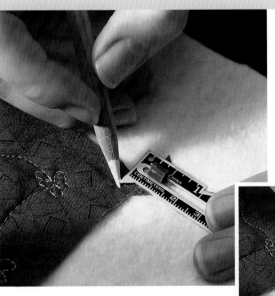

1

Determine the exact point at which the binding seam lines will intersect at each corner of your quilt top. **Use a 6-inch metal seam gauge to measure ¼ inch in from the edge of the fabric on both sides of the quilt top.** This becomes Point A. **Place a pencil mark at Point A.**

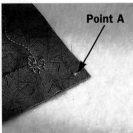

Point A

Tip

A 1 × 6-inch acrylic ruler can also be used to measure and mark Point A.

2

Begin stitching the binding to the quilt, taking care to start your stitching *away* from a corner. **Stitch the binding exactly to Point A, and do a few backstitches.** Stop, clip the threads, and remove the quilt from the sewing machine.

Tip

Backstitch exactly next to your original stitches, to the outside of the quilt (in the seam allowance).

3

Place the metal seam gauge at Point A (the point at which you stopped stitching), and measure from there to the folded edge of the binding fabric (Point B). Do *not* include the seam allowance. This measurement on your seam gauge (between Points A and B) becomes the distance you will use to determine the position of Point C.

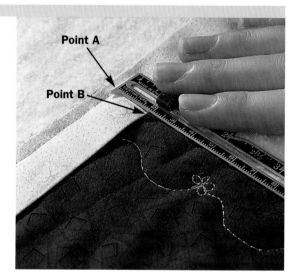

4

To locate Point C, reposition the seam gauge so that it extends from Point A out into the free end of the binding. Using the measurement from Step 3, **mark Point C with a pencil dot.**

Tip

Use a dark lead pencil on light fabrics and a white or light fabric-marking pencil on dark fabrics.

To make the corner fold, you will need to align Point C precisely with Point A. **Begin by inserting the tip of a silk pin through both layers of your binding at Point C.**

Holding the pin in the fabric at Point C, turn the binding so that you are able to insert the same pin into Point A (the point up to which the binding has already been stitched to the quilt) underneath the binding that has already been sewn on. Hold the pin up and down so that the points are aligned vertically.

Hold the pin straight up and down to keep Point C aligned exactly over Point A. The tip of the pin should pass through Points C and A. **Swing the unsewn strip of binding over so it aligns with the next (adjacent) side of the quilt.**

Tip

The binding will form an angled fold at the corner, between the layers of the binding.

MASTERING MITERS

8

Still holding the first pin straight up and down, **slide a second pin through the layers of the folded binding to hold it in place.** Remove the first pin. Position the quilt under the presser foot, being careful not to dislodge the fold. **Insert the sewing machine needle exactly at Point C.** Note: We removed the presser foot from the sewing machine so that you could see this technique clearly. You should, of course, sew with the presser foot on and in the down position.

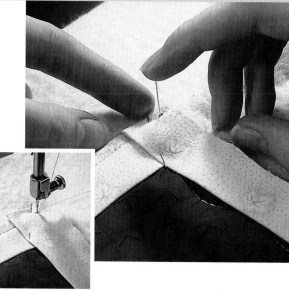
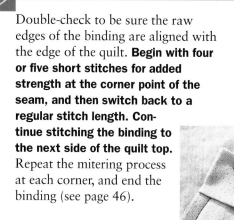

9

Double-check to be sure the raw edges of the binding are aligned with the edge of the quilt. **Begin with four or five short stitches for added strength at the corner point of the seam, and then switch back to a regular stitch length. Continue stitching the binding to the next side of the quilt top.** Repeat the mitering process at each corner, and end the binding (see page 46).

Hand Stitching Miters

1

Trim the backing and batting to your desired width. Fold the binding from the front to the back side of your quilt, and use silk pins to hold it in place. **Hand sew the binding to the backing fabric with a blind stitch, taking care to cover your machine-stitching lines as you work. Stitch up to the corner point, and stop.**

Tip

Steps 1 through 3 apply to right-handed quilters. Lefties should check Steps 4 through 6.

Fold the other corner of the binding in to meet the stitched binding exactly at the corner point. Use a pin to hold this folded edge in place. **Slide the needle gently inside the fold, up to the top of the miter.**

The folds on the front and back of the miter will naturally fall in opposite directions, creating a nice, flat look.

3

Using tiny whipstitches or blind stitches, stitch the mitered fold from the top down to the corner point. The thread in the photo is a contrasting color to make it easy to see these tiny stitches. **Continue stitching along the next straight edge of the binding on the adjacent side of the quilt.**

4

For lefties, the way the quilt is typically held to stitch the binding in place works against having the folds on the front and back of the miter naturally fall in opposite directions. **To compensate, stitch to within 2 inches of the corner. Knot and cut the thread.**

Tip

Instead of silk pins to hold the binding in place, try using binding clips. They're easy to open and won't prick your fingers.

MASTERING MITERS

5

Fold the adjacent side of the binding and pin it in position. **Stitch from the corner out about ½ inch. Knot and cut the thread.**

6

Return to the first side with the 2 inches that remain unstitched. Fold the edge down to complete the miter and pin it in place. **Stitch along the straight edge up to the corner, then slide the needle up inside the miter.** When it comes out at the outer corner of the miter, use tiny whip-stitches or blind stitches along the edge of the miter to stitch it closed. **At the bottom of the miter, slide the needle inside the binding along the ½ inch previously sewn, then resume stitching.**

7

After stitching the binding and mitered corners to the backing fabric, **stitch the mitered corner folds closed on the front side of the binding, using tiny whipstitches or blind stitches.**

Distortion Troubles

Problem	Solution
Finished binding looks cupped in on one or both sides of a mitered corner.	Perfectly square mitered corners need to have the binding stitched to the back side of the quilt evenly all the way up to the mitered areas, or the binding can pull out of shape. To help ensure this, do a test to check how evenly the binding will fold over to the back side of the quilt *before* you hand stitch it down. If necessary, trim a bit of seam allowance away to pare down some bulk, and when you're satisfied that the binding will fold over evenly, hand stitch it in place.
A diagonal seam in the finished binding falls too close to one of the mitered corners on a bed-size quilt.	The only sure way to know that this won't happen is to take the time to make a dry run and actually "walk" the prepared binding around the entire quilt by hand before stitching it to the quilt by machine. This way, you can determine a good starting point for attaching the binding and decide where to make adjustments, if any, to avoid the lumpy, misshapen look that results when seams are too close to a corner.

Skill Builder

Mitering corners at true 90 degree angles is easy with this innovative trick.

As you hand stitch the binding to the back side of a quilt, continue your stitching past the corner point (where you would normally stop to bring in the next side of the binding to form the mitered fold). Continue stitching *across* the seam allowance of the binding, all the way out to the folded edge of the binding on the next side of the quilt. This will make it easier to fold in the next side of the binding, and create a perfectly mitered corner.

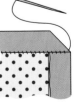

Try This!

You can stitch the mitered folds on both the back *and* the front sides of a quilt in one step. Stitch the miter closed on the back of the quilt as usual from the top of the corner; then push your needle through to the front of the quilt and stitch the front closed. When you've finished stitching the front miter closed, simply bring your needle through to the back side of your quilt at the corner point where the bindings meet, and you'll be ready to continue stitching the binding to the next side of the quilt.

I f you're hesitant to miter or want to expand your finishing horizons, here are two options: butted corners and rounded corners. Butted corners give you a square corner without the manipulations required for a miter. Rounded corners lend a gentler, more romantic feel to the quilt by softening the hard angles. When either of these choices is right for your quilt, use the following techniques for a problem-free application.

Getting Ready

Butted corners are a good choice when your binding fabric is patterned and may be difficult to match at a miter. They also make it easy to bind your quilt with more than one fabric, a popular look on country quilts. For butted corners, use straight-grain binding, either single- or double-fold, depending on your preference. The straight grain will help avoid distortion at the corners as you fold the ends closed. Prepare straight-grain binding as described on page 42.

Rounded corners are a graceful and logical finish for quilts with curves in the quilt design or border. Also, if a bed quilt extends to the floor, rounded corners prevent the quilt from being inadvertently stepped on. For rounded corners, use double-fold bias binding (see page 56) to best follow the curves. Measure the perimeter of the quilt, and cut and piece the binding 12 inches longer.

 *Thread color contrasts with fabric and markings are darkened in these photos for visual clarity.*

What You'll Need

- **Quilt, quilted and ready for binding**
- **Prepared binding**
- **Thread to match binding**
- **Rotary cutter, mat, and acrylic ruler**
- **Measuring tape**
- **Pencil or chalk**
- **Fabric scissors**
- **Silk pins**
- **Sewing machine**
- **Walking foot attachment or even feed feature**
- **Hand sewing needles**
- **Thread snips**
- **Saucer or plate for marking rounded corners**
- **Iron and ironing board**

Butted Corners

1

Measure through the center of your quilt in each direction. Prepare two pieces of straight-grain binding exactly the length of the longer measurement (for the sides of the quilt). Add 3 to 4 inches to the shorter measurement and prepare two pieces (for the top and bottom).

Pin the prepared binding to the two long sides. Match the raw edges of the binding to the straight quilt edge (see page 29). Match the ends of the binding to the ends of the quilt, easing the edge of the quilt, not the binding, as needed to fit. Sew the binding to the quilt, using a ¼-inch seam allowance.

Tip

If your quilt is square, bind two opposite sides, as described here, and then the two remaining sides, as described on pages 72–73.

2

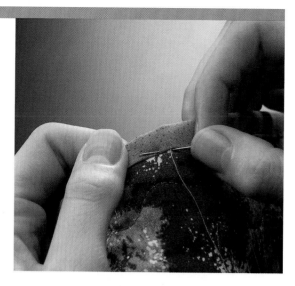

Trim the batting and backing from the long sides. Fold the binding over the layered quilt edge to the back of the quilt. **Position the folded edge of the binding to cover the stitching on the backing, pin in place, and hand sew the binding to the back of the quilt.**

Tip

Match the color of your thread to the binding fabric, not the backing, for invisible stitches.

3

Beginning about 1 inch from an end of one short binding strip, mark a pencil line across the strip. **From that mark, measure the length of your short side (from Step 1). Mark another line to indicate the short side measurement.** Pin the strip onto a short side, matching the raw edges of the binding to the marked straight quilt edge, **and matching your drawn lines on the binding to the cut edges of the quilt.** Ease the quilt top, not the binding, to fit as necessary. Sew the binding to the quilt, using a ¼-inch seam allowance and backstitching at each end. Repeat for the second short side.

4

Measure carefully from the pencil mark you made on the binding and mark ⅜ inch outside that mark. Trim the strip so that there is ⅜ inch remaining on the end. Repeat for the other end of the strip, and both ends of the other short strip.

Tip

Butt a cutting mat up against the completed bound edge to raise your binding strip up and provide a no-slip surface for marking.

Trim the batting and backing to your desired width. **Fold the excess ⅜ inch in so it lies on top of the binding strip.** Pinch the fold tightly and fold the binding over the layered quilt edge to the back of the quilt. **Sew the binding to the back of the quilt by hand, and tack down the folds at the corner of the quilt with invisible hand stitching.**

Double-fold binding makes the corners easier to manipulate when they are being turned to the back of the quilt.

Rounded Corners

The size of your quilt's curved corner will depend on what you use to draw the curve. **Remember to keep the size in scale with your quilt:** Use a saucer for a small wallhanging or baby quilt, a medium-size plate for a throw or lap quilt, and a dinner plate for a bed-size quilt. And keep in mind that your finished curve will be slightly smaller than your traced plate because of the ¼-inch seam allowance.

Prepare your quilt as instructed on page 29, including basting around the perimeter of the straight quilt edge. To mark the corner, lay the plate on the corner of your quilt. The edges of the plate should touch the straight quilt edge on both sides of the corner. **Trace the shape of the plate with a pencil.** Remove the basting stitches from the corner of the quilt, and **trim the quilt top along that marked line with fabric scissors.** Leave the batting and backing untrimmed for now.

Sew a line of basting stitches just inside your drawn curved corner, over-lapping the previous basting by about 1 inch on each end.

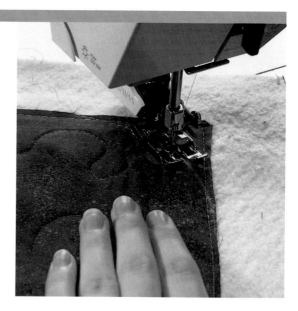

Starting at the side of the quilt a few inches from a corner, **pin double-fold bias binding so the raw edges are aligned with the straight quilt edge.** Take care not to stretch the bias. Stitch around the corners slowly using a ¼-inch seam allowance, easing any tucks or "burps" out of the way before they are caught in the stitching.

Trim the batting and backing to your desired width. Turn the binding over the raw edges of the quilt to the back. Position the binding so the folded edge just covers the stitching line.

Use a cool iron on the front of the quilt to **ease the edge of the binding at the corner so it lies flat without twisting or puckering.** Hand sew the binding to the back of the quilt.

The Quilter's
Problem Solver

Getting Flat Corners

Problem	Solution
Butted corners do not always lie flat or straight.	Problems with lumpy, bumpy butted corners are usually caused by bulk, either from the binding fabric or the batting. Try one or more of these solutions: ❑ Baste the extra ⅜ inch of binding in place before turning the binding to the back of the quilt. This will keep the binding corner straight and square. ❑ Trim out the underneath layer of the seam allowance. Removing the bulk—which won't show anyway—automatically makes it easier to create a flat corner. ❑ Trim the batting away from the corners before beginning to bind the quilt. ❑ Use a dressmaker's clapper to flatten the corner: Steam the corner; then place the clapper on the corner and hold firmly for several seconds, applying pressure to the corner.

Avoid the temptation to stitch your binding to the quilt without first pinning it in place.

Pinning will prevent the binding from becoming misaligned, either with the edge of the quilt or between layers of binding. The weight and drag of the quilt can cause an unsecured binding to be applied unevenly so that it stretches, twists, or puckers. Pinning takes a little time, but it will save time (and frustration!) spent correcting problems. And with butted corners, pinning allows you to match the edge of the quilt to the length of the binding, keeping your quilt very square.

Try This!

If a rounded corner appeals to you, think ahead. Plan your quilt so the design of either the quilt top, the border, or the quilting makes a rounded border seem not only logical but essential. Some possibilities:

❑ Pieced quilts with curved seams or an illusion of curves.

❑ Corner blocks adjusted so a curved inset of the border fabric can be added.

❑ Appliqué borders with curved motifs, such as vines, floral sprays, or swags.

❑ Quilting designs that curve around the corners, such as feathers, cables, flowers, and Celtic designs.

MASTERING OTHER CORNER FINISHES

Mitering
Uncommon Corners

Not all corners are square, as any quiltmaker can tell you. But some are intention-
ally deeper or shallower than the standard 90 degrees, like those on an octagonal
quilt. Some are even "inside out," with inverted 90 degree corners, like antique
reproduction quilts that leave room for the posts at the foot of the bed. With the techniques
showcased here, you can tackle any uncommon corner with confidence.

Getting Ready

Quilt your project by hand or machine. Square up the edges, marking your straight quilt edge (see page 29). Prepare enough binding to finish off your quilt (see pages 36–45 and 52–61).

The important thing to remember when mitering unusual corners—either inside or outside ones—is patience, patience, patience. Take your time when folding the miters, pin them carefully, and inspect both the front and the back of the quilt before you're satisfied with your miter. If it's a little off, unpin and refold it before proceeding. A little extra time up front buys you a much nicer miter in the end. And just think how gratifying it will be when your admirers notice (or don't!) your perfectly mitered corners.

 Thread color contrasts with fabric and markings are darkened in these photos for visual clarity.

Inside Corners

1

To miter an inside corner, you'll first need to find the point at which the binding should make its turn (this is where you'll form your miter). Lay a ruler along the edge approaching the inside point, lining up the width of your binding with the straight quilt edge. **Mark a line with a pencil at the corner. Repeat for the other side of your inside corner. The two lines will intersect at the turning point.**

Tip

You can mark the point with a pin so you can see it easily when sewing your binding on.

2

While sewing the binding to the quilt, shorten your stitch length for ½ inch heading into the turning point. **Stitch exactly to the turning point, and stop with the needle down exactly in the turning point.** Remove your marker pin, if you've used one, just before the needle approaches it. Note: We removed the presser foot so you could clearly see this technique. You should, of course, sew with the presser foot on and in the down position.

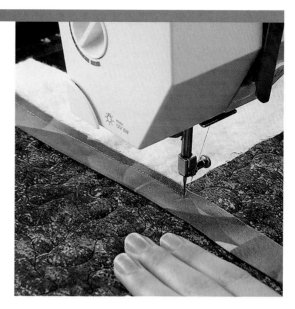

3

Lift the presser foot and turn the quilt so that the edge adjacent to the one you just stitched is lined up with the presser foot. Manipulate the edge you just stitched behind the presser foot so that the edges of the quilt going into and coming out of the inside point line up straight with each other. **The binding should lie flat and straight along the edge, and the quilt will bunch up beside the needle.**

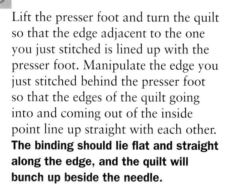

4

Lower the presser foot, and **continue the short stitches for another ½ inch before returning to a normal stitch length.** You should have short stitches going into and coming out of the corner. Continue stitching and mitering until your binding is sewn to the entire edge and the ends are joined.

 5

Trim your batting and backing to the desired width. **At each inside corner, notch the *binding only* from the outside raw edge into the marked turning point, stopping your clip just a couple of threads before the turning point.**

6

Turn the binding to the back of the quilt over all the layers. The notch in the binding allows the extra fabric to fall into natural miters on the front and back of the quilt. Stitch the binding to the backing using an invisible stitch. Sew the miters closed.

Tip

If your miter is lumpy or bunched, recut the notch to increase the size slightly.

Non-90-Degree Corners

1

Mark your turning point by following the instructions in Step 1 on page 77.

2

Begin sewing the binding to one side of the quilt. Continue sewing until you reach a turning point; stop with the needle down. **Pivot the quilt so that you are ready to sew along the next edge, and take one backstitch.** (The backstitch will angle away from your previous line of stitching.) Remove the quilt from the sewing machine. Note: We removed the presser foot so you could clearly see this backstitch. You should, of course, sew with the presser foot on and in the down position.

3

Fold the binding so that the edge of the strip extends parallel to the next edge you will sew. Place the fold so that it bisects (falls exactly in the middle of) the angled corner. Pin the fold along the angle to keep it intact. **Fold the binding again, aligning the binding's raw edge with the adjacent side of the quilt. Make this second fold in the top of the binding exactly at the corner of the quilt.** Pin the binding securely in place.

4

Sew the binding to the next side of the quilt, **backstitching over the seam intersection where the previous stitches ended.** Sew all corners in the same manner. When complete, fold the binding over to the back of the quilt and stitch in place using invisible stitches. **The folds at the corners will provide you with easy miters.** Sew the miters closed.

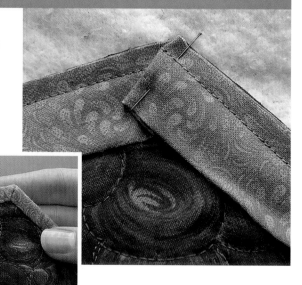

The Quilter's
Problem Solver

Achieving Attractive Miters

Problem	Solution
Mitered seams are off center.	The trick to centering miter seams on outside corners is in manipulating the binding fabric on the back of the quilt. Fold the binding to the back along both edges approaching the corner, stopping about 1 inch on each side of the corner. Tuck under one edge, then tuck the adjacent edge so that the fold on top splits the angle of the corner and appears to run straight through the angle. Check the angle of the seam on both sides, then pin securely in place before hand sewing the binding down and sewing the miter closed.
Mitered corners are bulky.	Extra pleats in the corners of the binding indicate there's extra fabric in the mitered corner. To get rid of the bulk, simply trim out the batting between the quilt top and backing at the corners. This will allow the needed extra room for the fabric in the pleats.

Skill Builder

Don't be intimidated by odd corners—make yourself a set of step-by-step examples!

Just as we have photographed samples in each step of binding here, you can do the same, and have your own set of samples that you can use to manipulate, practice on, and use for reference whenever you need to bind an odd-shaped sample. This way, once you get it right, you'll have each stage in front of you, and you'll never again have to think, "How did I do that?"

Try This!

If you just can't quite get the hang of mitering odd-shaped outside corners, try a wrapped-edge binding (see page 86). This method uses the backing as binding. After pressing under your raw edge, fold the backing to the front, and take the first fold directly perpendicular to the corner angle. Then, fold the sides in to form your miter, positioning the folds to meet so that they split the angle exactly in half.

MITERING UNCOMMON CORNERS

Finishing
without Binding

Sometimes the edge of your quilt speaks for itself. In that case, the best binding solution is often no binding at all! This chapter unveils two terrific no-binding alternatives. Each is a snap to do, requires no additional fabric, and gives a no-fuss, traditional appearance that is equally effective for straight and tricky curved or irregular edges.

Getting Ready

Two of the most time-honored methods for finishing a quilt without applied binding are the envelope and the turned-edge finish. In each case, the end result is that the quilt top and backing are tucked in and then secured with stitching for a crisp, sharp edge. However, the techniques used to get to this point are *very* different!

With the envelope method, you learn a new order of layering your quilt. The edges are completed before quilting, and the finishing is primarily by machine. If you need a quick edge finish on a wallhanging or smaller quilt, this is your dream come true.

The turned-edge method involves more handwork. You'll layer and baste as usual, but leave the outer ½ inch of your quilt un-quilted. This technique is suited to any size quilt and can be a simple way to finish the tricky edges on Tumbling Blocks and Grandmother's Flower Garden quilts.

 *Thread color contrasts with fabric in these photos for visual clarity.*

What You'll Need

Quilt top, batting, and backing (for envelope method)

Quilt, quilted and ready for edge finishing (for turned-edge method)

Thread to match quilt top

Tape measure or ruler

Fabric scissors

Silk pins

Sewing machine

Walking foot attachment or even feed feature

Hand sewing needles

Thread snips

Envelope Method

1

The envelope (or pillowcase) method differs from all other finishing methods in that the edges are finished *before* the quilt is quilted.

Square the quilt top as usual (see page 29), and trim the quilt top, backing, and batting even with the straight quilt edge. **Place the batting on the bottom; then place the backing *right side up* on top of the batting, carefully aligning the edges. Place the quilt top *right side down* to finish the quilt sandwich.** Be sure that the layers are smooth, flat, and wrinkle-free. Pin the edges securely to avoid shifting.

 Tip

For neatly aligned edges, cut the backing and batting a few inches larger than the top, then trim them after the quilt has been layered.

2

Position the layered quilt sandwich so that the wrong side of the quilt top is on top and the batting is on the bottom. Begin with a few back-stitches, and **use the even feed feature or walking foot attachment on your sewing machine to stitch around the perimeter of the quilt sandwich.** Start at the midpoint of one side of the quilt, and use a ¼-inch seam allowance.

Finish with a few backstitches, leaving an opening of 12 to 20 inches from the point at which you began stitching.

Tip

A good rule of thumb is to leave an opening of one-fourth to one-third the length of the side.

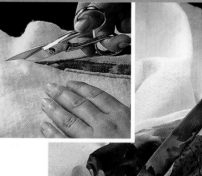

3

Trim the batting close to the stitching line, leaving approximately ⅛ inch beyond the stitching line. At the opening, trim the batting *even* with the stitching line. Do *not* trim the quilt top or backing.

Turn the quilt sandwich right side out by pulling it through the opening.

4

Finish the seam by turning the un-finished edge of the quilt top under ¼ inch.

Turn the backing under so that it aligns evenly with the edge of the quilt top and is folded over the batting. **Close the seam by hand with a blind stitch.** Use a matching or neutral thread to be certain that the stitching is truly invisible. Baste and quilt your quilt as desired.

Baste an envelope-finished quilt extremely well at the edges to make sure they don't roll as you quilt.

Turned-Edge Method

Also called the knife-edge finish, the turned edge is one of the oldest methods of quilt finishing.

To achieve the traditional turned-edge finish, layer and baste the quilt as usual. Begin quilting, but **be sure all quilting ends at least ½ inch from the desired finished edge.** Trim the batting and backing even with the straight quilt top edge; then **retrim the batting so that it is a little smaller (about ⅛ inch) than both the top and the backing.**

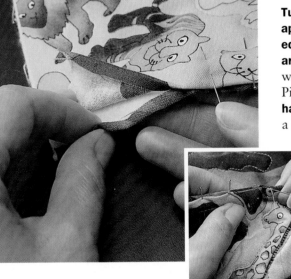

Turn the edge of the quilt top under approximately ¼ inch. Then fold the edge of the quilt back so that it wraps around the batting and is exactly even with the folded edge of the quilt top. Pin or baste the edges together; then **hand stitch the front to the back** with a blind stitch and matching thread.

Tip

Stay stitch or machine baste your quilt top and backing ¼ inch from your straight quilt edge before quilting to provide an easy turning guide.

Remove the pins or basting stitches; then **add a final line of quilting stitches ¼ inch from the edge of the quilt.** This added perimeter of stitching adds an attractive finishing touch, reinforces the edge, and prevents both the top and the back from shifting out of place.

FINISHING WITHOUT BINDING

Making Perfect
Wrapped-Edge Bindings

Wrapping the backing around to the front of the quilt is an easy way to go—with just a few simple steps, your quilt is bound, without the fuss of making binding strips and attaching them to the quilt. This also gives you a great way to showcase that "perfect" backing fabric that otherwise spends its life hidden against the wall or facedown on the bed.

Getting Ready

It is essential to plan for a wrapped-edge binding while you are planning your quilt, so that your backing fabric will coordinate both in color and in design with the front of the quilt. Also, you'll need to purchase enough yardage to allow for the extra fabric that will turn under and wrap around to the front.

When you piece and/or cut your backing, cut it large enough to allow for at least twice the width of your finished binding *on each side of the quilt.* (So, for example, for a ¼-inch finished binding, you'll need at least ½ inch extra backing on each side, measured out from your straight quilt edge.)

Using a nondirectional backing is usually your best bet. It takes an awful lot of fussing to get plaids, stripes, and other directional fabrics to look as if they were planned on a wrapped-edge binding.

 Thread color contrasts with fabric in these photos for visual clarity.

What You'll Need

Quilt, quilted and ready for edge finishing

Thread to match backing

Rotary cutter, mat, and acrylic ruler

Small square acrylic ruler

Pencil

Fabric scissors

Silk pins

Sewing machine

Walking foot attachment or even feed feature

Hand sewing needles

Thread snips

Wrapped-Edge Binding

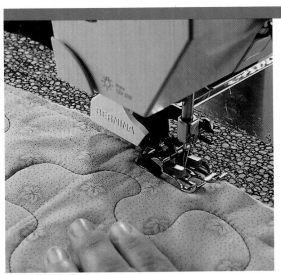

1

Trim the quilt top and batting even with the straight quilt edge. Do *not* trim the backing yet. **Machine or hand baste ¼ inch from the edge through all layers around the perimeter of the quilt.**

Tip

Slide your cutting mat between the backing and batting to prevent cutting the backing accidentally.

2

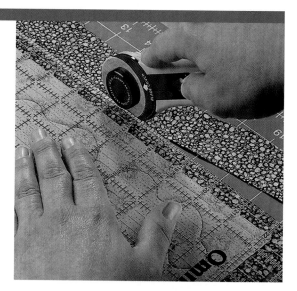

Trim the backing fabric to twice the width of your desired finished binding. In the quilt shown, the binding finishes at ¼ inch, so the backing is trimmed to ½ inch from the edge of the quilt top and batting.

Tip

Some quilts may call for a binding wider than ¼ inch. Don't hesitate to use ½ inch or even wider bindings for a decorative flourish.

3

On a square ruler, find the markings that correspond to the size of your finished binding. **Position the ruler on the corner of the quilt so that the diagonal line intersects the corner and the markings line up with the edges of the quilt.** Mark Point A at the corner of the ruler with a pencil dot.

Point A

4

Tip

Use the ruler to make sure the second crease is parallel to the first before you trim.

Fold the corner of the backing exactly across the corner of the quilt top, forming a right triangle. Gently finger press a fold in the backing. Take the tip of the triangle and fold it back until you can see Point A. Finger press this second crease. **Trim off the tip of the triangle that extends beyond Point A.**

5

Pin the fold in place. Use a long pin that lines up with both Point A and the corner of the quilt. **Bring one side of the back over to the front.** The folded edge at the corner should align with the diagonally placed pin. Repeat for the other side.

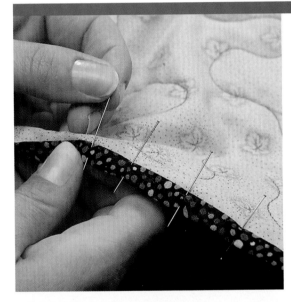

6

Turn the raw edge under, taking care to produce a smooth, even edge on the front of the quilt. **Pin the folded binding in place on the front of the quilt.**

Tip

Bias bars help you measure the finished binding before pinning to ensure a uniform width.

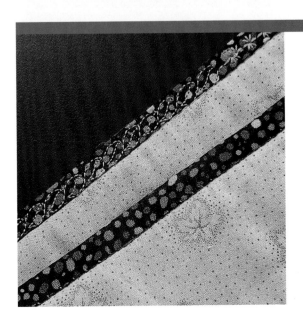

7

Sew the binding to the front of the quilt by hand or machine. Blind stitch the miters closed. Remove the basting stitches. If sewn by hand, add a row of quilting right along the edge of the binding to prevent the edges from shifting.

If sewing by machine, consider using some decorative stitches for a fun accent. The leaf and star stitches shown here are just a couple of possibilities. Place the stitches on the binding side so they come right up to the folded edge. Some stitches, like a feather stitch, can straddle the binding and quilt top.

Finishing
with a Facing

W hen dealing with a quilt with irregular edges—like diamonds, hexagons, or even scallops—what's a quilter to do? Just face it! Instead of applying a standard binding and turning all those tricky corners, borrow a technique from garment construction and attach a simple facing.

Getting Ready

After the facing is applied, it will be folded over to encase the raw edges of the quilt, then stitched down on the back, where it will overlap the backing fabric. Cut strips for the facing that are wide enough to wrap around and fully cover any inside points. Measure from the outermost point on the raw edge of the quilt top to the deepest inside point, then add 1 inch to that measurement. Measure the sides of your quilt, and cut facing strips that length plus twice the width of the strips. (For example, for a 96-inch side, cut 6-inch-wide strips that are 96 + 12 inches, or 108 inches long.) Press under ¼ inch of the long raw edge of each facing strip to get them ready to attach to the quilt.

▶ *Thread color contrasts with fabric in these photos for visual clarity.*

Facing a Quilt

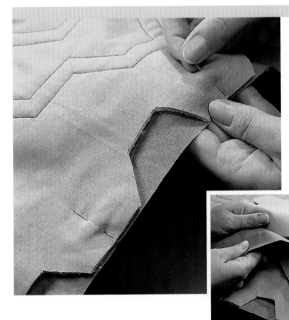

Prepare the backing for the quilt sandwich as normal, and quilt all the way to the outer edge. Carefully trim the batting and backing even with the edge of the quilt top. Place the facing strip on a flat surface, right side up. **Place the quilt top on the facing strip, right sides together. Make sure that there is at least ½ inch of facing fabric extending below the lowest inside points to provide ample coverage once the facing is turned to the back.** Pin all the layers together securely.

Tip

Select a facing fabric that contrasts with the backing for dramatic impact. Or use the same fabric as the backing to disguise the facing.

FINISHING WITH A FACING

2

With the quilt on top and the facing underneath, sew through all layers and attach the facing strip to the quilt side. Sew the facing strips to opposite sides first, then to the top and bottom. Use a ¼-inch seam and a walking foot or even feed feature, and follow the shape of the edges as you sew.

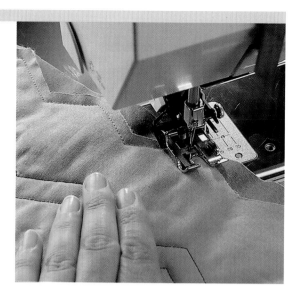

3

As you approach an inside point, switch to a short stitch length for about 1 inch before and after the point. These tight stitches will make the angled portions of the seam less likely to come apart over time. They also reinforce areas where you will be trimming closely.

When you get to the end of a side, **stop stitching ¼ inch from the corner** so you can miter the facing on the back of the quilt later (see Step 5 on the opposite page).

4

On each side, trim the facing even with the edge of the quilt top. **For inside points, trim to within ⅛ inch of the short stitches, being careful not to clip into the stitches.** The less bulk there is in the seam, the smoother your facing will lie. **For outside points, trim off the tip of the point** to lessen the bulk.

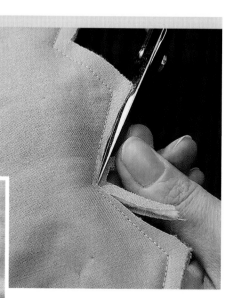

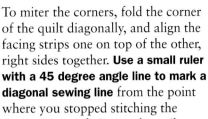

To miter the corners, fold the corner of the quilt diagonally, and align the facing strips one on top of the other, right sides together. **Use a small ruler with a 45 degree angle line to mark a diagonal sewing line** from the point where you stopped stitching the facing to the quilt top out to the edge of the strip. Sew the miter, and **trim ¼ inch outside your sewn seam.** Repeat for all corners.

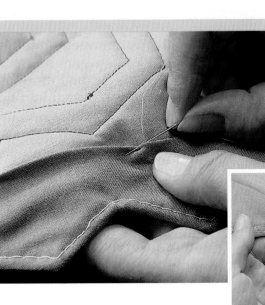

Turn the trimmed facing to the back of the quilt. Make sure the seam is at the edge of the quilt, or slightly to the back, so the facing won't show on the quilt front. Smooth the edge so that it lies as flat as possible. **Hand or machine baste the facing in place, basting very close to the edge of the quilt.**

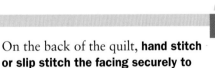

Tip

Use a wooden Popsicle stick or the end of a chopstick to smooth the angles on the turned facing.

On the back of the quilt, **hand stitch or slip stitch the facing securely to the back of the quilt.**

To keep the edge of the quilt from shifting or rolling, sew a row of quilting along the edge. Place your stitches ¼ to ½ inch from the finished edge. **Remove the basting stitches.**

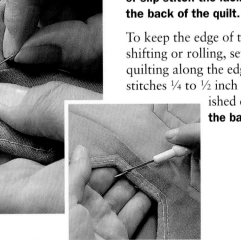

Sensational
Scalloped Edges

M any quilts, such as Double Wedding Ring, have naturally occurring scalloped edges. On other quilts, you may cut scallops along the border for a purely decorative accent. Whether they're natural or created, scalloped edges create a pretty, classy profile for the edge of your quilt. Binding these curves, with their ins and outs, is simple if you know a few tricks.

Getting Ready

Binding for scallops must be cut on the true bias. This will allow the binding to stretch around the curves while remaining flat along the edges. Even with bias, deep scallops (half-circles) are tricky to bind. Consider re-designing them so they are shallower and take less of a "bite" at the V (inner point).

To determine the length of bias binding needed, measure your quilt by laying a piece of string along the scalloped edges. To this length add another 10 inches. Double-fold binding can be easier to maneuver along the curves and points because you don't have to deal with the loose folded-under edge that comes with single-fold binding. Single-fold binding, however, presents less bulk to turn over along the edges. Experiment to see which one is easier for you.

Thread color contrasts with fabric and markings are darkened in these photos for visual clarity.

What You'll Need

Quilt, quilted and ready for binding

Prepared bias binding

Thread to match binding

Acrylic ruler

Pencil

Fabric scissors

Silk pins

Sewing machine

Walking foot attachment or even feed feature

Binding Scallops

1

Baste the three layers of your quilt together securely ⅛ inch inside the marked or natural scalloped edge. This will prevent the curved edges from stretching when you apply the binding. **Cut the quilt top, batting, and backing along the drawn scalloped line.** If your quilt has natural scallops, trim the batting and backing even with the quilt top after basting.

Tip

If you are adding scallops to a straight border, mark and cut them before attaching the binding.

2

Place a pencil mark ¼ inch inside each V. With scissors, clip through all three layers, stopping just before the mark. Clip straight into the V from the edge of the quilt. Be very careful not to clip up to or through the mark.

Tip

On a bed-size quilt, you may prefer to mark and clip one edge of the quilt at a time.

3

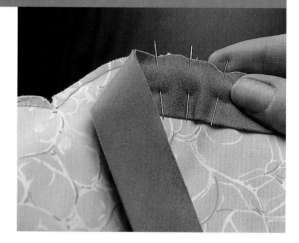

Begin pinning the binding to the front of the quilt at the top of a curve, away from a V. Lay the binding along the scallop gently, being careful not to stretch it. Align the cut edges of the binding with the scalloped edge of the quilt top.

Place the pins perpendicular to the quilt edge. As you pin, ease the fullness of the binding along the sewing line. The eased fabric will later help the binding turn over the curve and lie flat when it is finished.

Tip

Pinning from the front allows you to evenly distribute the binding along the curves and Vs. You will sew from the back.

4

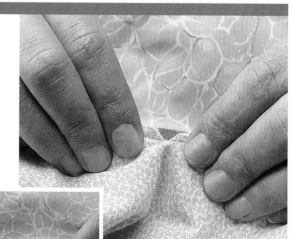

When you get to the V, spread the scallops apart so they form a straight line. Still working from the front of the quilt, pin the binding along the edge, placing one pin on each side of the V. **Make sure the top two corners of the clipped V align with the straight edge of the binding.** Continue pinning the binding along the next scallop and V.

Stitch the binding to the quilt with the backing facing up and the binding (and pins) on the bottom. This makes it easier to stitch a straight line across the Vs and to avoid puckers. Slide the pins out of the way just as the needle approaches. Stitch a ¼-inch seam, guiding the presser foot along the raw edge. Be careful not to pull on and stretch the scallops.

When you get to a V, spread the scallops apart gently and stitch in a straight line across the base of the V. Keep the stitching to the outside of the clipped area. Note: We raised the presser foot in the inset photo for clarity; please sew with the presser foot down.

Tip

If you get a pucker in the binding, release a few stitches before and after the pucker, then restitch.

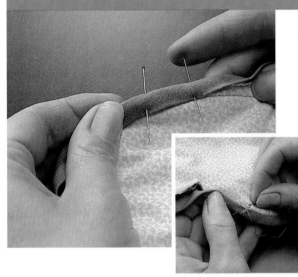

Turn the binding to the back of the quilt, one curve at a time. **Beginning at the top of a curve, fold the binding over the edge so that it meets the stitching line.** Pin in place. **Blind stitch the binding in place,** stopping about 1 inch before the V.

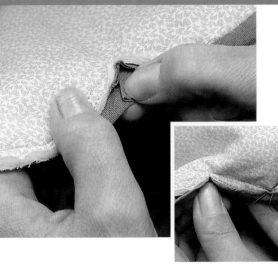

To miter the inner point, fold and pinch the binding at the V. Gently bring the miter over the edge of the quilt with your thumb, matching the fold to the point of the V on the back. Pin the miter at the V. Pin the unstitched area, matching the binding edge to the stitched line. Blind stitch the binding, taking several stitches at the mitered fold to secure it.

Continue pinning and stitching along the curves and Vs of the scallops.

Quick-and-Easy
Prairie Points

Prairie points make a charming finish—but they require a lot of time and inclination to cut, piece, fold, pin, and stitch individually to a quilt. The results can be stunning, but who has the time? Luckily, you can get almost the same look with much less work with continuous prairie points. This nifty technique streamlines the cutting and positioning steps for points in a flash.

Getting Ready

Prairie points are an inserted edge finish, which means that they are sandwiched between the quilt top/batting and the backing. When quilting a project that will be finished with prairie points, leave 1 inch unquilted along the edges.

To prepare for attaching the prairie points, trim the batting and backing even with the straight quilt edge. Then baste the top and batting together, leaving the backing free.

If you want to get a head start on the final finishing step, fold under and press ¼ inch all along the raw edge of the backing.

 Thread color contrasts with fabric and markings are darkened in these photos for visual clarity.

Continuous Prairie Points

The height of your prairie points is your first consideration. Make sure that they will be in scale with your overall design—very large prairie points will look out of place on a quilt made of tiny pieces. Points over 2¾ inches high tend to flop over; tiny ones get lost on large quilts.

To calculate the width of the strip you'll need, **add ¼ inch to the desired finished height of your prairie point, then multiply by 4.** (For a 2-inch-high point, cut your strip 2 + ¼ = 2¼ inches, times 4 = 9 inches wide.) The length is variable; you'll get as much length as your yardage allows.

Tip

Strips of 10 to 12 prairie points are easiest to handle.

2

Tip

The easy formula for marking your cutting lines is "strip width divided by 2."

Cut the fabric strip, fold it in half lengthwise with wrong sides together, and press the fold. Unfold and position the strip so the fold runs up and down (not side to side) on your work surface. On the right side of the pressed line, begin at the bottom and **measure off and mark segments equal to one-half your strip width.** Draw the cutting lines from fold to outer edge.

On the left side, start one-half segment from the bottom (in this example, begin 2¼ inches from the bottom edge). Then continue to mark full-size segments, measuring up from the half-segment line.

Tip

Don't use a rotary cutter for this step— you need to stop *exactly* at the pressed line.

Using fabric scissors, cut from the outside edge on each side along your drawn lines, stopping at the pressed fold in the center. Cut out the half-segments at the top and bottom of the left side.

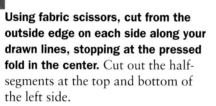

Working on your ironing board for convenience, begin folding the prairie points. Start at the bottom of your strip, and **fold the bottom square on the right side in half diagonally by taking the bottom right corner up to meet the top left corner.**

Still working on the same square, **fold it in half diagonally again** by taking the top right corner down to meet the bottom left corner. Pin the bottom point of your prairie point.

For the second and all following squares, the sequence is slightly different.

Move to the opposite side of your strip. (If you just folded a prairie point on the right side, you'll fold one on the left side next.) Make the first fold as you did for the previous step. **Then flip the completed prairie point from the right side over on top of the prairie point that is half folded.** Make your second diagonal fold in the second prairie point, nesting the first point *into* the second one. **Pin the bottom point of the second prairie point, securing the nested point.**

After the first point has been folded, remember: Fold once diagonally, flip the previous prairie points over to that side, then fold diagonally again.

Continue folding and nesting your cut strips in this manner until your entire strip is folded. Make enough short strips (10 to 12 prairie points) to equal the total length you will need to go around the perimeter of your quilt.

Machine baste the prairie points into one long strip, sewing ⅛ inch from the raw edge. Nest each set of prairie points into the previous set as you sew, spacing it to match the others. Remove the pins as you sew.

Tip

Feed the strips into the machine fold-first so the fold doesn't open up.

8

To finish the edge, pin the prairie points to the right side of the quilt top, matching the raw edges. **Fold the backing out of the way and sew the prairie points to the quilt top and batting using a ¼-inch seam.**

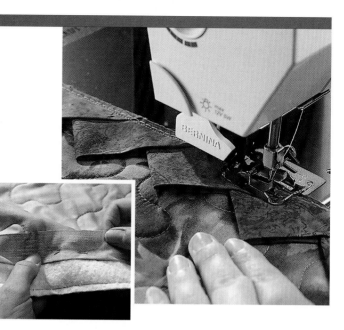

9

Flip the prairie points out, away from the center of the quilt. Press gently. Fold and press under ¼ inch of the raw edge of the backing, and **hand stitch to the prairie points.**

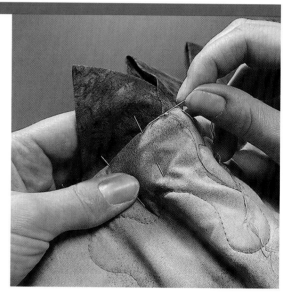

10

Once your backing is sewn on, you can **add additional quilting at the edge if desired.**

Two-Color Continuous Prairie Points

1

To add variety and excitement to your prairie point edge, add a second color! The technique is the same as for continuous prairie points—you just need to prepare a two-color strip.

Cut two strips, one of each color to alternate in the prairie points. To calculate the width of the strips you'll need, **add ¾ inch to the desired finished height of your prairie point, then multiply by 2.** (For a 2-inch-high point, cut your strip 2 + ¾ = 2¾ inches, times 2 = 5½ inches wide.)

2

With *wrong* sides together, sew the strips together, using a ¼-inch seam. **Press the seam to one side; then mark, cut, fold, and baste as directed in Steps 2 through 7 on pages 100–101.** Follow Step 8 on the opposite page to sew the prairie points to the quilt.

Note: On two-color continuous prairie points, the finished base of the triangles is ½ inch from the raw edge. Allow for that extra when you are positioning your prairie points to sew them to the quilt.

Tip

To reduce bulk at the edge of your quilt, trim the seam allowance down to ¼ inch before sewing the prairie points to the quilt.

3

Finish the quilt as directed in Steps 9 and 10 on the opposite page.

QUICK-AND-EASY PRAIRIE POINTS

T hink of cording as fabric icing and of your quilt as the cake. Adding a thin line of color along the edge of the quilt brings a distinctive touch of dimension and definition. Covering cotton cording with bias-cut strips of fabric doesn't take much extra time or effort, and attaching it is easy.

Getting Ready

Cording, sometimes called filled piping, is made by covering cotton cording with bias-cut strips of fabric. It is an inserted edge, so leave the outer ½ inch of your quilt unquilted. To determine how much cording to prepare, measure the perimeter of the quilt and add 12 to 15 inches. Choose a technique from "All the Basics on Bias Binding" on page 36 to cut and piece a continuous bias strip.

Strip width depends on the thickness of the cording. After wrapping strips around the cord, a total of ½ inch must remain for the seam allowance. It's best to cut strips a little wider than necessary, so that the seam allowance can be trimmed back to exactly ¼ inch when assembly is complete. Strips 1¼ inches wide work well for #18 cording, a commonly used size. Keep the scale of your project in mind when selecting the cord width.

 Thread color contrasts with fabric in these photos for visual clarity.

Adding Cording

1

Fold the bias strip in half lengthwise and finger press it slightly, wrong sides together. You don't need a sharp crease, just enough of a fold to help establish a channel for the cording. **Lay the cording into the crease, and wrap the fabric over it snugly, matching the raw strip edges as closely as possible.**

Tip

For extra zing, use striped fabric. The bias-cut stripes will add lots of movement.

2

Use a zipper foot to machine sew a basting stitch along the length of the cording. Place one side next to the cording as you sew. Stitch the seam close to the cord, but leave just enough space to insert another row of stitching between the cording and the basting later. Match the strip edges carefully as you work.

3

Remove the cording strip from the machine. Place your acrylic ruler on top of the strip, with the ¼-inch rule aligned just inside the seam—the spot where a second seam will be stitched when the cording is sewn to the quilt. **Trim the cording seam allowance to a consistent ¼-inch width.**

4

If your cording must wrap around curves, make a series of clips from the raw edge of the strip almost to the seam line. You can add more clips later, if necessary for a good fit, or cut out small V-shaped sections of the seam.

Trim the quilt top, batting, and backing even with the straight quilt edge. **Beginning midway along one side, place the cording on top of the quilt, raw edges together, aligning and pinning several inches at a time.** Leave a 1-inch tail at the beginning point.

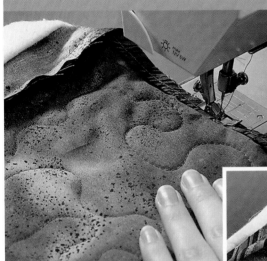

Move the batting and backing out of the way. **Use matching thread to sew the cording strip to only the quilt top, placing the new seam between the first seam and the cording.** Stop and pin short lengths of the strip to the quilt as you work. **For neatly turned corners, make perpendicular clips in the seam allowance of the cording strip, beginning just before each corner and continuing past it.** At the corner, stop with your needle down, take one or two stitches across the corner for a neater turn, then continue up the other side of the quilt.

Stop sewing about 2 inches from your starting point. **Fold the fabric back from your starting tail to expose the cording, and clip the cording off about ½ inch inside the end (not the fold) of the fabric;** leave the fabric intact. Lay the ending tail flat and clip the cord and fabric so they are flush with the starting cording.

Unfold the starting fabric over both tails. Tuck the raw edge of the starting tail fabric under, pin it, and finish sewing the cording to the quilt top.

Finish the backing as described in Steps 9 and 10 on page 102.

Adding
Decorative Piping

S ometimes just a sliver of color does wonders to frame or define a portion of a quilt. A bright, contrasting fabric sewn between a dark border and binding accents the division between the two. Or you can use a neutral color as a bridge between fabrics that may not work as well together when placed side by side. Piping is made by simply folding a strip of fabric. It's a great way to accent an area without introducing extra bulk.

Getting Ready

Piping can be made from either bias or straight-grain strips of fabric. Sew piping strips into a continuous length using one of the binding strip assembly methods given on pages 36–45. To determine strip length, measure the length of each area where piping will be used; then add 2 inches or so for insurance.

Decide how much piping width should be visible in the finished piece—a narrow bead of color or a wider swath for a bolder look. If the perimeter of your quilt is surrounded by blocks, consider how the overlapping piping will affect their appearance.

Use this simple formula to determine the beginning strip width: desired finished piping width times 2 + ½ inch = beginning strip width.

Thread color contrasts with fabric in these photos for visual clarity.

What You'll Need

Quilt, quilted and ready for binding

Prewashed, pressed cotton fabric for piping

Thread to match piping fabric

Prepared binding

Rotary cutter, mat, and acrylic ruler

Fabric scissors

Silk pins

Sewing machine

Walking foot attachment or even feed feature

Hand sewing needles

Thread snips

Iron and ironing board

Using Piping with Applied Binding

1

Press the piping strip in half lengthwise, wrong sides together. To avoid stretching the piping, use an up-and-down pressing motion, rather than dragging the iron back and forth across the strip.

Use bias-cut piping strips when you want to adorn curved and scalloped edges.

A D D I N G   D E C O R A T I V E   P I P I N G

2

Pin a folded piping strip to each side of the quilt, raw edges aligned with the straight quilt edge. Strip ends should overlap and extend approximately 1 inch past each corner. For square corners, each piping intersection should form a 90 degree angle.

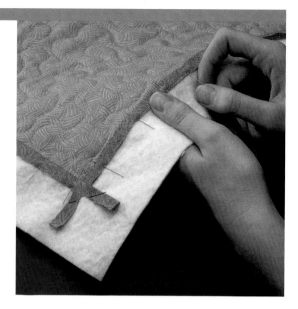

3

Align the raw edge of your prepared binding with the raw edge of the piping, and use a consistent ¼-inch seam allowance to sew the binding to the quilt. Remove the pins holding the piping to the quilt as you reach them. These precautions will help you achieve a piping that's the same width all the way around.

4

Trim the batting, backing, and excess ends of piping strips as described on page 29. **Turn the binding to the back of the quilt and pin it in place so that it covers all the layers.** Stitch the binding to the back of the quilt by hand.

Once you finish your binding, your piping is visible on the front of your quilt, between the border and the binding.

Using Piping with Wrapped-Edge Binding

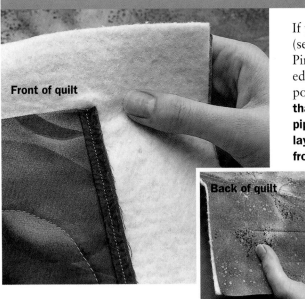

Front of quilt

Back of quilt

If you prefer a wrapped-edge binding (see page 86), you can still use piping. Pin the piping strip to the quilt's edges as shown in Step 2 on the opposite page. **Using a bobbin thread that matches the backing, sew the piping to the quilt through all three layers. End each seam exactly ¼ inch from the adjacent straight quilt edge** (where the two lines of stitching will intersect).

Trim the quilt top, batting, and backing as described beginning on page 86. **Fold the backing and blind stitch the folded edge to the front of the quilt, taking the stitches through the piping and the quilt top.** Use a thread that matches the backing. Make sure the folded edge meets the piping uniformly all the way around the quilt.

ADDING DECORATIVE PIPING

Adding a
Hanging Sleeve

Y ou've worked so hard on your quilt, you're fully entitled to show off your workman-
ship. Whether your quilt will hang in your living room or at a quilt show, be sure
that it will hang securely by adding a sturdy hanging sleeve. And, if you're displaying
it at home, we've included several quick, easy, low-cost alternatives to purchased commercial
hangers.

Getting Ready

A hanging sleeve or pocket is used to display a quilt on a wall or other vertical surface. It is usually made from fabric, and either sewn permanently onto the back of a quilt (for wallhangings) or attached temporarily (for a bed quilt to be hung in a show). Use sturdy fabric that can hold the weight of the quilt; loosely woven plaids, for example, should be avoided.

When selecting a hanger to display your quilt, you can turn to one of the many commercially available hangers (available through quilt shops and mail-order catalogs). Or if you want to spend a little less (and have more to spend on fabric!), try one of the ideas at the end of this chapter.

 Thread color contrasts with fabric in these photos for visual clarity.

Permanent Hanging Sleeve

1

Most quilt shows require a 4-inch-wide hanging sleeve. Since that is also a fairly accommodating size, the instructions that follow will yield a 4-inch sleeve. To make a wider sleeve, cut a wider piece of fabric.

Cut a strip of fabric 9 inches wide across the width of your fabric. The length of your strip should be 1 inch shorter than the width of your quilt.

If your quilt is wider than 40 inches, piece strips together to get the length you need, and press those seams open.

Tip

Permanent sleeves are attached after the quilt is quilted, but before it is bound.

2

Stitch the seam allowances down using matching thread. This keeps the hanging rod from catching in the loose fabric. Use either a straight stitch about 1/16 inch from the raw edge or a zigzag stitch just at the edge.

Hem the short ends by turning under 1/2 inch and stitching them down as you did the seam allowances.

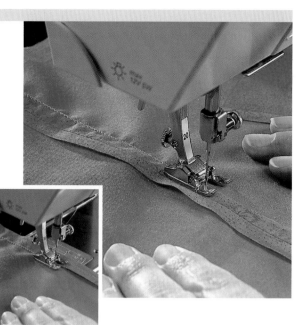

Tip

Use a decorative stitch on your machine to hem the edges for a fun, fancy flourish.

3

Fold the sleeve in half lengthwise, wrong sides together. **On the back of the quilt, align the raw edges of the sleeve with the line of basting that you have sewn along the straight edge of your quilt** (see page 30). Pin the sleeve in place.

Tip

If you are finishing with a method other than applied binding, use the temporary method on the opposite page instead of this permanent method.

4

Sew the sleeve to the quilt through all layers, sewing *inside* the 1/4-inch seam allowance. This way, when you bind the quilt, those stitches will be hidden inside the binding's seam allowance.

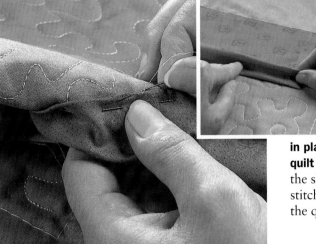

Instead of letting the sleeve lie flat against the quilt back, **make a small pleat in the tube, taking up about ½ to ¾ inch of fabric.** This allows some space for the rod to pass through. **Pin the bottom edge of the sleeve in place and sew it to the back of the quilt by hand.** Sew the short ends of the sleeve to the quilt. Make sure no stitches show through to the front of the quilt.

Temporary Hanging Sleeve

To make and attach a temporary sleeve that can be easily removed, follow Steps 1 and 2 on pages 113–114. Fold the tube in half lengthwise, wrong sides together, matching long raw edges. **Sew along the long edge, using a ½-inch seam allowance.** Press the seam open.

Center the seam on one side of the tube and pin the hanging sleeve seam side down on the back of your quilt, just underneath the binding at the top of the quilt, and about 1 inch inside each side of the quilt. Using thread that matches the front of your quilt, sew the top of the sleeve to the quilt. **Every couple stitches, sew through all layers of the quilt.** This avoids excess tension on the back of the quilt, which can pull it out of shape.

3

Finish sewing the bottom edge of the sleeve to the back of the quilt as directed in Step 5 on page 115.

4

For very large quilts, such as bed quilts, make multiple short sleeves instead of one long one. These smaller sleeves distribute the weight more evenly and reduce stress on the backing.

For very small quilts, such as miniatures, make narrower sleeves. Cut your strips 6 inches wide for a sleeve that finishes at 2½ inches.

Inexpensive, Easy Quilt Hangers

1

The simplest hanger is a plain wooden dowel. To make it invisible, cut it ½ to 1 inch longer than your hanging sleeve. After you insert it into the sleeve, the protruding ends of the dowel can hide behind the edges of your quilt, with the ends resting on nails pounded partway into the wall.

To make your dowel into a decorative element, cut it about 2 inches longer than the width of your quilt. **Tie matching cording to each end so it can hang from one centered nail, or glue or tack wooden shapes to the ends and rest the ends on nails.**

Curtain rods make excellent quilt hangers. **For fairly lightweight quilts, a standard thin (⁵⁄₁₆ inch), round, adjustable metal rod is a good choice.** It can slip into the hanging sleeve and rest on two nails just like a dowel.

For larger, heavier quilts, a thicker rod (⁷⁄₁₆ inch) and hanging brackets are in order. Mount the brackets onto the wall, slip the rod into the pocket, and place the ends of the rod in the brackets.

A third option is a **U-shaped curtain rod,** which stands out from the wall several inches. These rods mount to the wall and allow air to circulate behind the quilt, which is especially useful in humid climates.

Instead of buying an expensive combination hanging rod/shelf, make your own. Purchase an unfinished country-style shelf from a craft store. It should be slightly longer between its supports than the width of your quilt. **Drill ⁵⁄₈-inch holes through the supports, and slide a purchased ½-inch dowel through the holes.**

Sand and finish the shelf and rod before you hang the quilt so that the quilt doesn't snag on any rough edges.

Tip

To prevent splintering, drill most of the way through the support from one side, then finish from the other side.

If you must hang a heavy quilt on nails but you're worried about a single dowel supporting the weight, try this trick. **Purchase inexpensive ½-inch electrical conduit from a home-improvement store.** Cut it to the same length as you would an invisible dowel (see Step 1 on the opposite page), and tape the ends with duct tape (to avoid snagging the sleeve). Insert the conduit into the hanging sleeve, string clear fishing line through the conduit, and tie the ends of the line in a loose loop. This arrangement will support a large quilt on only one centered nail, and guarantees a sag-free quilt.

Tip

If your home-improvement or hardware store won't cut the conduit for you, purchase an inexpensive conduit cutter for yourself.

Quilt Labeling
Made Easy

*T*ake the time to make a label. With this simple step you vault yourself from anony-
mous quiltmaker to an actual person, immortalizing your place in the world of quilts.
After all the time you've spent pondering color and fabric, piecing, quilting, and
binding—what's another hour or so? Pause to put the story of your quilt where it won't get
lost and where it will travel with the quilt on the rest of its journey. The techniques high-
lighted in this chapter are particularly quick and easy, so you have no excuse not to label!

Getting Ready

Before you design your label, decide how much information you want to include. This will affect how large you make the label. For true documentation, you should include the who (maker and receiver), the what (the quilt's name and background), the where (city, state, possibly country), the when (include starting and ending dates, if desired), and the why (occasion).

Pay particular attention to the kind of pen you use. You'll want an ink that is permanent, goes on smoothly and easily, and won't harm the integrity of the fabric. Don't use a regular ballpoint pen or a permanent marker, like a Sharpie. The pens mentioned in the text are all recommended for label making.

Some wonderful books provide ready-made designs for you to trace. See the resources on page 126 for information on ordering books with ideas for labels.

See the resources on page 126 for information on ordering books with ideas for labels.

What You'll Need

- **Quilt, finished and bound**
- **Fabric for label**
- **Thread (to match label fabric; decorative)**
- **Acrylic ruler**
- **Permanent fabric markers**
- **Fabric scissors**
- **Silk pins**
- **Sewing machine**
- **Walking foot attachment or even feed feature**
- **Freezer paper**
- **Light box**
- **Hand sewing needles**
- **Thread snips**
- **Fusible web**
- **Stamps and fabric ink**
- **Stencils**
- **Fabric paint and small paintbrush**
- **Iron and ironing board**

Simple Labeling Techniques

Quick and Easy

The absolute fastest way to label your quilt is to write directly on the backing. Besides speed, this documentation has the advantage of never separating from the quilt. Use a fine-tip permanent pen, such as a Pigma, and include as much information as you would on a label. Spread the quilt flat and use your other hand to spread the fabric as smooth and taut as possible to make writing on the layered quilt easier. Heat set the pen ink by pressing with a dry iron, covering the writing with a plain piece of muslin first.

Tip

Practice rough drafts of the wording and spacing on lined paper before you take pen to fabric.

Cut a piece of freezer paper the same size as your desired finished label, plus an extra ½ inch all around. **With a fine-point Sharpie and acrylic ruler, draw parallel guide lines on the dull side of the freezer paper where you wish to write.** Press the shiny side of the freezer paper to the wrong side of the label fabric. The dark lines will show through as a writing guide so the lines of information you write will be straight and evenly spaced. **Use a permanent fabric marker for the lettering.**

2

Tip

If you're not the greatest at freehand lettering, label design books often provide alphabets for tracing. Skip Step 1 and trace the lettering as described here.

Add decorative borders around the lettering. There are a number of books with label designs meant to be traced, or you can create your own border. **Place the design over a light box and the label fabric over the design.** (Peel off the freezer paper backing from the label so you can see the design for tracing.) Tape the label fabric so there is no slippage. Trace the outline of the design, using a permanent fine-tip fabric pen. **When you are finished, remove the fabric, place it over another piece of fabric to stabilize it, and go over the lines to darken them if necessary.**

3

Tip

For very cute, no-trace labels, buy screen-printed designs from Block Party Studios. Color the designs and you're done! See the resources on page 126.

Add any color or shading with wider-tip permanent fabric pens, such as Identipens. Place the label over another piece of fabric to stabilize it if it tends to move around while you are coloring. Heat set the pen ink by pressing with a dry iron, covering the label with a plain piece of muslin first.

Trim any excess fabric from your label, leaving ¼ inch extending beyond the design. **Press the ¼ inch to the wrong side of the label along all the edges.** For neater corners, press the corners in toward the center of the label first, forming "dog ears." Then fold and press the adjacent sides, creating a miter.

For labels with no inked decorative borders, here's an easy way to add a colorful finishing touch. **Machine stitch along the edge, using decorative stitches and decorative thread.** Adjust the size of the stitch so that it suits the size of your label.

Pin the prepared label onto the back of the quilt. **With a thread that matches the label fabric, blind stitch the label onto the quilt.**

Tip

For a completely permanent label, attach it to your backing *before* you quilt, then quilt through it.

Fast Fusing 1

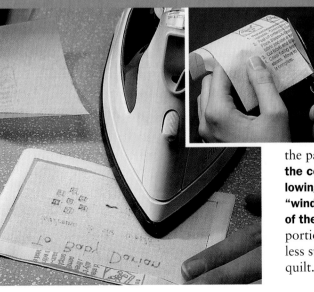

Use fusible web as a quick-and-easy way to anchor a label to your quilt. Trim your inked and colored label to the desired finished size. Cut a piece of fusible web to the same size. Draw a line ⅜ inch inside all the edges on the paper side of the web. **Cut away the center portion of the web, following the drawn lines. Press this "window" of fusible web to the back of the label.** Trimming out the inner portion of the web makes the label less stiff once it's attached to your quilt.

QUILT LABELING MADE EASY

2

Peel away the paper layer and fuse the label to the back of your quilt. Follow the manufacturer's guidelines for heat setting and timing. Too much heat or heat applied for too long a time can cause the edges of the fusing to separate from the quilt.

3

Fusing also gives you an easy way to dress up a plain label. Make the basic label from muslin or a light-colored tone-on-tone fabric. Pick a motif from a print fabric and press fusible web to the wrong side. **Cut out the motif, peel off the paper backing, and fuse onto the label fabric.** Repeating a motif from a fabric on the front of the quilt adds a nice finishing touch.

Stamping

Tip

Quilt shops, quilt-supply catalogs, and craft stores carry fabric ink. Also, check the resources on page 126 for Wallflower Designs.

Stamping produces quick, elegant labels. With the new fabric inks, you can use any rubber stamp on fabric. **To ink the stamp, hold the stamp up and the ink pad down.** This allows you to see how much ink is applied to the stamp. Tap the ink pad lightly several times onto the stamp (rather than squishing it hard). Light tapping prevents over-inking the stamp. **Stamp on a smooth, flat surface.** Press down firmly, without rocking the stamp from side to side.

Complete and attach the label as described under "Trace and Stitch" on page 120 or "Fast Fusing" on page 121.

Stenciling isn't just for walls—it's an easy way to make beautiful labels. Use fabric paint, a stencil brush, and a tiny stencil to create a border or corner designs for your label. Purchase these supplies at a craft shop or quilt shop.

Tape your fabric to a table or other flat surface. Hold small stencils in place by hand, or use masking tape to stabilize larger ones. **Dip the brush into the paint and rub the paint onto the fabric in small circular motions.** Let the paint dry, then heat set it with a dry iron, covering the paint with a clean piece of muslin first.

The secret to good stenciling is to use a scant amount of paint. The bristles should be barely damp.

Computerized Labels 1

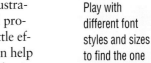

Most word processors now let you easily produce a beautiful label. Make use of the fancy typefaces, rainbow of colors, and library of clip art illustrations that come with your word processing program. With only a little effort, your personal computer can help you create a label that's exactly the size you need and contains all the information and designs you want to include.

You can print out the computer-generated design and trace it onto your label fabric (see "Trace and Stitch" on page 120). Or you can let technology take you to the next step.

Tip

Play with different font styles and sizes to find the one that you like best.

2

Once you've designed the label on the computer, print out your creation. Cut a piece of freezer paper to $8\frac{1}{2} \times 11$ inches. Iron the wrong side of your label fabric to the shiny side of the freezer paper. Trim the fabric to the size of the freezer paper. Feed this into your printer, and print out the label as usual. (On most computer/printer setups, the "single sheet" setting works best.) Peel away the freezer paper, place the label between clean sheets of paper, and press to heat set the ink.

Tip

Test your printer with scrap fabric to be sure it can handle processing the thickness of the label.

QUILT LABELING MADE EASY

Finishing *Glossary*

A

Applied binding. A binding cut from a separate piece of fabric, then sewn to cover the edges of the quilt.

B

Backing. The plain or decorative panel used on the back side of a quilt.

Basting. The process of temporarily securing the layers of a quilt together to keep them from shifting during an assembly process.

Batting. The filling placed between the quilt top and backing.

Bias. A 45 degree angle to the straight grain in a piece of fabric.

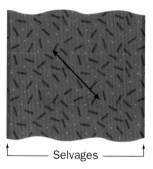

— Selvages —

Bias binding. Any binding with edges cut along the bias grain of the fabric.

Binding. A long, narrow strip of cloth that covers the raw edges of a quilt.

Binding clips. Barrettelike metal clips that snap shut to secure the folded binding to the back of the quilt during final hand sewing.

Blind stitch. An invisible hand stitch used for appliqué and other finish work.

Butted corner. A corner finish in which the binding strips end and overlap at each corner of the quilt.

C

Continuous bias binding. A long bias binding cut from a specially prepared tube of fabric. This technique avoids having to piece individual bias strips together to create a long length of binding.

Cording. A three-dimensional, decorative trim made by surrounding cable cord with bias strips of fabric; used as an inserted edge finish.

Crosswise grain. The grain formed by threads that run perpendicular to the selvages.

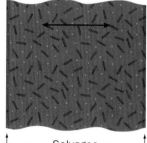

— Selvages —

D

Directional print. A distinct, one-way motif, such as stripes.

Double-fold binding.
Double-fold binding. Binding that covers quilt edges with two layers of fabric; made by folding a binding strip in half lengthwise.

E

Envelope finish. An edge finish created by sewing around the edges of a quilt and its backing, placed right sides together, then turning the unit right side out before completing the seam.

Even feed feature. A feature on many sewing machines that works in conjunction with the feed dogs to advance all layers of a quilt at the same rate. *See also* Walking foot attachment.

F

Facing. An edge finish made by sewing a frame of fabric face down around the quilt edges, then turning and sewing it to the backing.

Filled piping. Another name for cording.

French-fold binding. Another name for double-fold binding.

H

Hanging sleeve. A permanent or temporary tube of fabric on the quilt back that provides a place for inserting a dowel or other hanging device.

Inserted binding. A binding that is cut from a separate piece of fabric, then sewn between the layers at the edge of the quilt.

K

Knife-edge finish. Another name for a turned-edge finish.

L

Label. A permanent or temporary message telling the history of the quilt and the quiltmaker.

Lengthwise grain. The grain created by threads that run parallel to the selvages in a piece of fabric.

— Selvages —

M

Mitered corners. A corner finish in which the binding strip is continuous and turns the corner of the quilt, making a small pleat at the corner.

P

Pillowcase finish. Another name for envelope finish.

Piping. A decorative trim made from folded strips of fabric, inserted between the edge of the quilt and the binding.

Prairie points. Decorative triangles made from folded fabric squares; an inserted edge finish.

R

Rounded corner. A curved corner constructed and cut from an originally square corner.

S

Scalloped edge. A series of curves, either drawn on the edge of the quilt or naturally occurring, such as in a Wedding Ring quilt.

Single-fold binding. Binding that covers the quilt edges with a single layer of fabric.

Self binding. A binding made from a portion of the quilt or backing, rather than one applied from a separate length of fabric.

Straight grain. The lengthwise or crosswise threads in the weave of fabric.

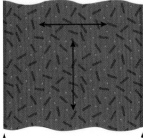

— Selvages —

Straight-grain binding. Binding strips that are cut with edges parallel to the fabric's straight grain.

Straight quilt edge. The marked edge of the quilt that will serve as the finished edge once the quilt is bound.

T

Turned-edge finish. A self binding made by folding under and matching the edges of the quilt and the backing, then blind stitching them together.

W

Walking foot attachment. A presser foot with a mechanism that works in conjunction with the feed dogs to advance all layers of a quilt at the same rate. *See also* Even feed feature.

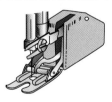

Wrapped-edge binding. A self binding made by folding the backing to an even width, folding it to the front of the quilt, and stitching it in place.

Resources

Block Party Studios
1128 Tenth Street
Nevada, IA 50201
(515) 382-5232
Screen-printed label designs

ReadyBias
1747 Spyglass Lane
Moraga, CA 94556
(888) 873-2427
100% cotton ready-to-use continuous binding

Wallflower Designs
Box 307
26210 Royal Oak Road
Royal Oak, MD 21662
(410) 745-0135
Stenciling and label supplies

About the Writers

Mimi Dietrich is well known for her finishing finesse. She is actively involved in quilt research with the Smithsonian Institution's National Museum of American History.

Dixie Haywood is the author and coauthor of several books on quilting. An award-winning quilt-maker, Dixie specializes in topics as wide-ranging as precision piecing and crazy piecing.

Becky Herdle is a quilt author, teacher, lecturer, and certified judge who always makes time to quilt. Her work has been published in numerous quilting magazines, books, and calendars.

Susan McKelvey is a well-known quiltmaker, teacher, lecturer, and author. She runs Wallflower Designs, which distributes books, patterns, and supplies for quilters.

Ann Seely and **Joyce Stewart** are award-winning quilting sisters. They teach around the country and recently turned their most popular class, *Color Magic for Quilters*, into a book for Rodale Press.

Janet Wickell specializes in miniature quilts but teaches a variety of quilting topics around the country. She is a freelance quilt writer and has recently authored a book on quilting.

Darra Duffy Williamson is a frequent contributor to quilting magazines; she travels extensively, teaching and lecturing at quilt guilds and shows. She was named Teacher of the Year in 1989.

Acknowledgments

Quiltmakers

Elsie Campbell, Pharaoh's Phans on page 82
Sharyn Craig, Paper Chain on page 25
Mary Dowling, Serpentine Horizon on the cover and pages 2, 21, and 94
Kaffe Fassett and **Liza Prior Lucy,** Yellow Pennants on page 98
Susan Horn, Pennsylvania Amish on the cover and on page 21
Nancy Johnson-Srebro, Star Flight on page 52 and Dresden Star on page 116
Christine Klinger, Tertulia on the cover and on page 21
Susan McKelvey, Color Wheel on page 27 and Amish Baskets on page 27
Judy Murrah, Jacket Jazz quilt on the cover and pages 10 and 21
Suzanne Nelson, Feathered Summer Star on page 24, My Stars on page 26, and Sophie's Orchard Star on page 26
Mabeth Oxenreider, Plaid Colorwash Houses on page 76
Sue Phillips, Planet Windows on page 25
Piece o' Cake Designs, Rainbow Garden on page 104
Ursula Reikes, Dinosaurs on page 26 and Bzzzz on page 36
Sally Schneider, Apple Orchard on pages 6 and 56 and MT TRiangled on page 24
Anita Shackelford, Friendship's Flowering on page 108
Eloise Smyrl, Climbing the Wall on page 70
Karen Soltys, Group Therapy on pages 23 and 24 and Golden Delicious on page 31
Debbie White, Yo-yo's Garden on page 90

Sample Makers

Barbara Eikmeier, Susan McKelvey, Suzanne Nelson, Sally Schneider, and Jane Townswick

Fabric and Supplies

American & Efird—thread
Bernina of America, Inc.—sewing machine
Dream World Enterprises—Sew Steady sewing table
Olfa/O'Lipfa—rotary cutters
Omnigrid, Inc.—rotary cutting mats and rulers
Warm Products, Inc.—batting
Benartex, Kaufman, Mission Valley, and P&B—generously donated fabric

Index

INDEX